MATHEMATICS IN FOCUS, K-6

How to Help Students Understand Big Ideas and Make Critical Connections

Jane F. Schielack
and
Dinah Chancellor

HEINEMANN
PORTSMOUTH, NH

Heinemann
361 Hanover Street
Portsmouth, NH 03801–3912
www.heinemann.com

Offices and agents throughout the world

The authors and publisher wish to thank those who have generously given permission to reprint borrowed material:

"100 or Bust!" from *Explorations: Uncovering Math with Manipulatives, the TI-10, and the TI-15 Explorer* by Jane F. Schielack and Dinah Rice Chancellor. Copyright © 1995. Published by Texas Instruments Incorporated. Reprinted by permission of the publisher.

"Focal Points" and excerpt from *Curriculum Focal Points for Prekindergarten through Grade 8 Mathematics: A Quest for Coherence* by the National Council of Teachers of Mathematics. Copyright © 2006 by the National Council of Teachers of Mathematics. Reprinted by permission of the publisher.

The Curriculum Focal Points identify key mathematical ideas for these grades. They are not discrete topics or a checklist to be mastered; rather, they provide a framework for the majority of instruction at a particular grade level and the foundation for future mathematics study. The complete document may be viewed at www.nctm.org/focalpoints.

Library of Congress Cataloging-in-Publication Data
Schielack, Jane F.
   Mathematics in focus, K–6 : how to help students understand big ideas and make critical connections / Jane F. Schielack and Dinah Chancellor.
      p. cm.
   Includes bibliographical references.
   ISBN-13: 978-0-325-02578-0
   ISBN-10: 0-325-02578-9
   1. Mathematics—Study and teaching (Elementary)—United States—Standards. 2. Sixth grade (Education)—Curricula—United States—Standards. 3. Curriculum planning—United States—Standards. I. Chancellor, Dinah. II. Title.
   QA135.6.S4185 2010
   372.7—dc22   2009043358

Editor: Victoria Merecki
Production editor: Patricia Adams
Typesetter: Eric Rosenbloom, Kirby Mountain Composition
Cover design: Bernadette Skok
Manufacturing: Steve Bernier

Printed in the United States of America on acid-free paper
14 13 12 11 10   VP   1 2 3 4 5

Contents

Acknowledgments ■ V

Introduction ■ VII

CHAPTER 1   Focusing the Curriculum by Building Purposeful
Connections: A Model from Nature ■ 1

CHAPTER 2   Designing Focused Instruction and Assessment: A Lesson
Template ■ 9

CHAPTER 3   Asking Targeted Questions to Focus on Foundational
Understandings: A Lesson on Whole Number Concepts
■ 20

CHAPTER 4   Identifying Priorities in a Focused Curriculum: A Lesson
Integrating Number and Measurement Concepts ■ 32

CHAPTER 5   Balancing Accountability and Sense Making in a Focused
Curriculum: A Lesson on Place Value ■ 50

CHAPTER 6   Connecting Representations to Focus on Deepening
Understanding: A Lesson on Multiplication of Whole
Numbers ■ 64

CHAPTER 7   Using Resources Thoughtfully to Focus Instruction:
A Lesson on Area Measure ■ 76

CHAPTER 8   Beyond Worksheets: A Lesson on Connecting Geometry
             and Measurement   ■   88

CHAPTER 9   Differentiating Instruction in a Focused Curriculum:
             A Lesson on Ratio and Rate   ■   106

CHAPTER 10   Reflecting on Ways to Support Focused Instruction:
             Lessons Learned   ■   121

APPENDIX A   Planning Tree   ■   130

APPENDIX B   Lesson Plan Template   ■   131

APPENDIX C   Kindergarten Lesson Plan: Let's Make Five   ■   134

APPENDIX D   Grade 1 Lesson Plan: So *Now* How Long Is It?   ■   143

APPENDIX E   Grade 2 Lesson Plan: 100 or Bust!   ■   149

APPENDIX F   Grade 3 Lesson Plan: Modeling Multiplication   ■   158

APPENDIX G   Grade 4 Lesson Plan: Area: Why Multiply?   ■   168

APPENDIX H   Grade 5 Lesson Plan: Prisms from Cubes   ■   175

APPENDIX I   Grade 6 Lesson Plan: Just Right!   ■   183

References   ■   190

Acknowledgments

This book is dedicated to all of the teachers who have touched our lives: the teachers who taught us to love school and to love mathematics; the teachers to whom we are married—Vince and Ray; the teachers who taught our children—Laura, Vince, Jeff, and Jon; the teachers who are teaching our grandchildren—Amanda, Kimmy, Nick, Ian, and Adam; the teachers with whom we taught—in Victoria, Waco, Denton, Bryan, and College Station, Texas; and the teachers we taught together in Bryan and College Station. We combined the qualities that made each of them memorable to create the teachers in the chapters of this book.

We deeply appreciate the teachers and principals in Texas who allowed us to borrow their classes to try out our lessons—in the Carroll school district, in the Midway school district, and especially in the Kerrville school district: Barbara Walther, Cathy Moretich, Darla Pfiester, Gwynne Fikes, Christie Yanez, Melissa Douglass, Carrie Overby, and Carolyn Herring; and their instructional leaders: Deb Wells, Amy Billeiter, Wade Ivy, Diane Stern, and Buck Thompson. We learned much from their students. The warm welcome from daughters-in-law, Michelle and Angie, made this part of the process possible. We also would like to express our appreciation to Kendra Beasley, the graphic designer who so expertly translated our image of learning and teaching as a type of ecosystem into a visual reality.

Finally, a special thank you goes to Emily Birch for initiating the idea of this book and to Victoria Merecki and Patty Adams and all the others at Heinemann who saw it through to completion.

—Janie Schielack
—Dinah Chancellor
Winter, 2009

v

Introduction

In this book, we will introduce you to the idea of teaching within a focused mathematics curriculum and offer you a variety of practical strategies for implementing lessons that support it. The defining characteristic of instruction within a focused mathematics curriculum is that teachers provide students with experiences that promote deeper understanding of core concepts, or big ideas, as well as with extended time to develop these complex understandings. This approach to teaching and learning mathematics satisfies a number of important needs:

- the teacher's need for *more effective and efficient use of instructional time* (particularly since there is not enough time to cover all of the separate pieces in a skill-a-day approach);
- the students' need for *opportunities to make the purposeful connections* that lead to important mathematical principles and generalizations; and
- the students' need for *experiences that build the depth of understanding* of the mathematical principles and generalizations that are required for doing well in higher-level mathematics, such as algebra.

In addition, when students spend more time at each grade level on learning experiences that are designed to deepen their understanding of critical concepts, teachers no longer need to revisit in isolation topics that were addressed in depth in earlier grades or to play superficially with topics that will be addressed in depth in later grades.

The Need for Focus in the Mathematics Curriculum

Mathematics in some form has been a major component of the elementary school curriculum for generations. Yet as recently as thirty years ago, there was very little guidance regarding the mathematical topics that students were expected to learn at each grade level. Individual schools or districts may have set certain benchmarks, but there was no requirement for the existence of these benchmarks or for determining whether or not students reached the benchmarks. As well, there were no standards by which to judge whether or not students were well equipped for understanding the world mathematically when they graduated from high school. In reality, educational settings existed in which teachers taught little or no mathematics, which left many students with a deficit as they entered the working world.

As a result, whether for good or ill (and often a mixture of both), external requirements for accountability of mathematics teaching and learning came into existence beginning in the 1980s. In particular, national, state, and district committees created sets of curriculum standards describing the expectations for the mathematics that should be taught and learned at each grade level (or at least by the end of a certain band of grade levels). Legislation mandated the design and implementation of accountability measures to verify that students were learning the mathematics. States and districts have been expected to use the feedback from the accountability measures to review the effectiveness of their mathematics curricula and to revise accordingly.

Because the development of mathematics curricula was directly connected to the call for accountability, many (maybe even most) mathematics curriculum documents in existence today closely resemble the test specifications used by test developers to create very specific assessment items. Elementary mathematics curricula are usually collections of tersely worded phrases, each narrow in scope and isolated from one another in order to make the assessment of each *piece* of understanding as direct as possible. An example of student objectives from this type of mathematics curriculum presentation might look like the following:

Number Sense

- Read and write whole numbers up to 1,000,000.
- From a place-value model, identify and write whole numbers up to 1,000,000.
- Round to the nearest ten, hundred, and thousand whole numbers up to 10,000.
- Use symbols for *less than, equal to,* and *greater than* to order and compare whole numbers.
- Rename and rewrite whole numbers as fractions.
- From objects or pictures, name and write mixed numbers.
- From objects or pictures, name and write mixed numbers as improper fractions.
- Write tenths and hundredths in decimal and fraction notations.
- Round two-place decimals to tenths or to the nearest whole number.

Computation

- Use efficient addition and subtraction algorithms to find whole number sums and differences.
- Represent any situation involving repeated addition as multiplication.
- Represent any situation involving the sharing of objects or the number of groups of shared objects as division.
- Demonstrate mastery of the multiplication tables for factors from one through ten.
- Demonstrate mastery of the corresponding division facts.
- Use efficient algorithms to multiply two-digit numbers by one-digit numbers.
- Use efficient algorithms to divide two-digit numbers by one-digit numbers.
- Understand the special properties of zero and one in multiplication.
- Use objects or pictures to add and subtract simple fractions with like denominators.
- Use objects or pictures to add and subtract simple fractions with unlike denominators.

- Use objects or pictures to add and subtract decimals (to hundredths).
- Use efficient algorithms to add and subtract decimals (to hundredths).
- Estimate results of any whole number computations.

In addition to the fact that pieces of understanding in most current mathematics curricula are listed in a disjointed fashion, they are also often sorted into strands such as Number, Operation, Algebraic Reasoning, Geometry, and Measurement. For example, a mathematics curriculum for grade 4 often includes an objective about factors and multiples in the Number strand, an objective about multiplication facts in the Operation strand, an objective about finding area in the Measurement strand, and an objective about solving number sentences such as $3 \times ? = 9$ in the Algebraic Reasoning strand. These objectives are all closely related mathematically to one another. However, it is difficult to note their relationships when they appear in such a curriculum document scattered over several pages, each one connected to separate assessment specifications. A mathematics curriculum that is presented in a disjointed form based on test specifications does not communicate the many connections among these pieces that are essential for students to make. Without these connections, students cannot develop the complex understandings that ensure future success in mathematics and related fields of knowledge.

An Example of a Focused Mathematics Curriculum

The National Council of Teachers of Mathematics (NCTM) recommends a more focused curriculum in elementary mathematics in order for students to build critical complex understandings. *Curriculum Focal Points for Prekindergarten through Grade 8 Mathematics: A Quest for Coherence* (NCTM 2006) proposes an approach to the presentation of the elementary mathematics curriculum that involves emphasizing the connected structure of the mathematics being learned rather than delineating isolated skills to be assessed. In the publication, NCTM presents an example of a mathematics curriculum that consists of three focal points at each grade level, along with a description of connections that link the focal points within a grade to each other and to focal points in prior and following grades. Figure Intro–1 shows an example of the focal points and connections for grade 4 (NCTM 2006, 16).

Curriculum Focal Points and Connections for Grade 4

The set of three curriculum focal points and related connections for mathematics in grade 4 follow. These topics are the recommended content emphases for this grade level. It is essential that these focal points be addressed in contexts that promote problem solving, reasoning, communication, making connections, and designing and analyzing representations.

Grade 4 Curriculum Focal Points	Connections to the Focal Points
Number and Operations and Algebra: **Developing quick recall of multiplication facts and related division facts and fluency with whole number multiplication**	*Algebra:* Students continue identifying, describing, and extending numeric patterns involving all operations and nonnumeric growing or repeating patterns. Through these experiences, they develop an understanding of the use of a rule to describe a sequence of numbers or objects.
Students use understandings of multiplication to develop quick recall of the basic multiplication facts and related division facts. They apply their understanding of models for multiplication (i.e., equal-sized groups, arrays, area models, equal intervals on the number line), place value, and properties of operations (in particular, the distributive property) as they develop, discuss, and use efficient, accurate, and generalizable methods to multiply multidigit whole numbers. They select appropriate methods and apply them accurately to estimate products or calculate them mentally, depending on the context and numbers involved. They develop fluency with efficient procedures, including the standard algorithm, for multiplying whole numbers, understand why the procedures work (on the basis of place value and properties of operations), and use them to solve problems.	*Geometry:* Students extend their understanding of properties of two-dimensional shapes as they find the areas of polygons. They build on their earlier work with symmetry and congruence in grade 3 to encompass transformations, including those that produce line and rotational symmetry. By using transformations to design and analyze simple tilings and tessellations, students deepen their understanding of two-dimensional space.
Number and Operations: **Developing an understanding of decimals, including the connections between fractions and decimals**	*Measurement:* As part of understanding two-dimensional shapes, students measure and classify angles.
Students understand decimal notation as an extension of the base-ten system of writing whole numbers that is useful for representing more numbers, including numbers between 0 and 1, between 1 and 2, and so on. Students relate their understanding of fractions to reading and writing decimals that are greater than or less than 1, identifying equivalent decimals, comparing and ordering decimals, and estimating decimal or fractional amounts in problem solving. They connect equivalent fractions and decimals by comparing models to symbols and locating equivalent symbols on the number line.	*Data Analysis:* Students continue to use tools from grade 3, solving problems by making frequency tables, bar graphs, picture graphs, and line plots. They apply their understanding of place value to develop and use stem-and-leaf plots.
Measurement: **Developing an understanding of area and determining the areas of two-dimensional shapes**	*Number and Operations:* Building on their work in grade 3, students extend their understanding of place value and ways of representing numbers to 100,000 in various contexts. They use estimation in determining the relative sizes of amounts or distances. Students develop understandings of strategies for multidigit division by using models that represent division as the inverse of multiplication, as partitioning, or as successive subtraction. By working with decimals, students extend their ability to recognize equivalent fractions. Students' earlier work in grade 3 with models of fractions and multiplication and division facts supports their understanding of techniques for generating equivalent fractions and simplifying fractions.
Students recognize area as an attribute of two-dimensional regions. They learn that they can quantify area by finding the total number of same-sized units of area that cover the shape without gaps or overlaps. They understand that a square that is 1 unit on a side is the standard unit for measuring area. They select appropriate units, strategies (e.g., decomposing shapes), and tools for solving problems that involve estimating or measuring area. Students connect area measure to the area model that they have used to represent multiplication, and they use this connection to justify the formula for the area of a rectangle.	

16   Curriculum Focal Points for Prekindergarten through Grade 8 Mathematics

Figure Intro–1   NCTM Curriculum Focal Points, Grade 4 (reprinted with permission)

Compare the disjointed, fragmented list of student objectives in the previous section to the presentation of similar content in the NCTM Curriculum Focal Points in Figure Intro–1. In the NCTM presentation, the individual pieces are packaged in a way that more directly supports instructional planning by relating them to a complex mathematical idea appropriate for that grade level. For example, "fluency with whole number multiplication" is presented in the NCTM Curriculum Focal Points as a major grade 4 learning goal that combines ideas from the Number and Operations and Algebra strands and is supported by appropriate pieces of learning, such as selecting and applying appropriate methods of estimation and calculation with various numbers of digits in the factors. As another example, the grade 4 NCTM Curriculum Focal Points presents "connections between fractions and decimals" as a major learning goal supported by the related ideas of representing equivalent fractions and decimals with a variety of models, including the objects, pictures, and symbols on the number line.

As a result of organizing the smaller learning goals around bigger ideas and refining the content in a single grade level to be more focused on the bigger ideas, the presentation of a mathematics curriculum in the manner of the NCTM Curriculum Focal Points differs quite a bit in length and specificity from the presentation in the bulleted list. In this book, we offer practical suggestions that teachers can use with their local and state mathematics curricula, no matter how it is currently organized, to realize the vision presented in NCTM's Curriculum Focal Points. In other words, we suggest a way to develop the big picture of mathematics in terms of the complex understandings that are expected to emerge in a given grade level with connections to complex understandings in previous and succeeding grade levels.

Creating a Focused Mathematics Curriculum

An instructional environment consisting of input from the public, the school district, a teacher, and students all involved in the design and implementation of curriculum, instruction, and assessment is an example of a *complex system*. To plan effective instruction, the teacher must make decisions that are driven by the multiple interactions among student needs, district standards, public expectations, and their own content knowledge and pedagogical expertise. Therefore, the science of complex systems can pro-vide us with a helpful analogy for justifying a focused curriculum as a solu-tion to the problem of creating efficient and effective mathematics learning. One important characteristic of a successful complex system is *synergy*. As Corning (2002) notes, "Broadly defined, synergy refers to *the combined (cooperative) effects that are produced by two or more particles, elements, parts or organisms—effects that are not otherwise attainable*" (26).

Synergy produces *emergent structures*, patterns not created by a single event or rule. In mathematics, a concept such as place value might be con-sidered an emergent structure. We can use an emergent structure in nature to help explain the complexity of developing the understanding of such a mathematical concept. Consider a tree, for instance. The growth of a tree requires a seed and specific elements in the soil, water, air, and climate. However, nothing *requires* the complex system of the forest environment to form the tree from the mere existence of these parts. (Imagine how many seeds fall in a forest that do not result in a tree!) Instead, the interaction of each part with its immediate surroundings causes a complex chain of processes leading to some order. Similarly, a tree cannot be created simply by joining a trunk, some branches, and some leaves. Again, it is the critical connections among these parts that provide the complexity needed to make a tree. In general, an emergent structure in a complex system is more than the sum of its parts. The emergent structure will not arise if the various parts are simply coexisting; the interaction of these parts is key.

Based on our complex systems analogy, what we need in order to address our current curriculum issues in elementary mathematics is some-thing we might call *curricular synergy*—a purposefully organized conjunc-tion and interaction of pieces of the curriculum in which the resulting emergent structures (complex mathematical understandings) are greater than the mere accumulation of those pieces. Curricular synergy acts as the powering force behind an instructional environment that promotes the emergence of complex understandings—such as place value—from a multiplicity of interactions between relatively simple experiences—such as making groups of ten, counting by tens, and identifying patterns in a hun-dreds chart. Organizing the mathematics curriculum around a few major areas of focus each year, along with the connections among these major areas (as exemplified in the NCTM Curriculum Focal Points), is a way to create this curricular synergy. Ideally, a state or district will organize its curriculum to generate this synergy; however, individual teachers also have opportunities for building curricular synergy within their own instructional environments.

In this book, we present the complex structure of a tree as a visual model teachers can use for building curricular synergy and designing a focused curriculum that highlights the development of complex understandings. Remember that a tree is greater than the sum of the separate elements in the environment (seed, soil, water, air, sunlight) and the resulting parts of its growth (trunk, branches, leaves). In the classroom, teachers aim to support the emergence of students' complex mathematical understandings by purposefully organizing strategies for instruction and conjunction of pieces of the curriculum that allow for the result to be greater than just the accumulation of those pieces in isolation.

How This Book Can Help You Implement a Focused Mathematics Curriculum

The decision to teach a focused curriculum will take special efforts in planning. Development of ideas across grades, connections between ideas across topics, and practice of skills in meaningful contexts are important components of a focused mathematics curriculum. To address the issues of depth and connections, each lesson in a focused curriculum must be designed with an eye on the prize. In other words, it must be built around a rich task that provides a context for the thoughtful questioning that leads students to the development of the desired complex understandings and related skills. Throughout this book, we offer a variety of techniques that all stem from the goal of *building purposeful connections* in order for teachers and students to be able to make sense of the myriad bits and pieces that exist in most mathematics curricula today when presented as lists of separated concepts and skills. Chapter 1 provides some suggestions for long-term planning, including guidelines for using a tree as a visual representation of the connections and depth involved in a given complex understanding.

Chapter 2 introduces a Lesson Template for designing instruction that supports a focused curriculum. Teachers can use the Lesson Template to plan instruction that highlights the purposeful connections related to the content of the lesson; includes strategies for accessing students' previous experiences and current understandings; identifies questions that focus student attention and assess learning; and offers techniques for bringing instruction to a close in ways that help students strengthen their understandings.

The remaining chapters highlight a range of strategies for designing elements of curriculum and instruction that impact students' formation of purposeful connections, including:

- prioritizing and combining mathematical ideas within tasks;
- making thoughtful selections of instructional tools, including technology;
- building relevance for mathematics through meaningful settings;
- managing classroom conversations;
- building connections among multiple representations;
- allowing appropriate time for revisiting ideas;
- using assessment to identify student needs; and
- differentiating instruction based on student needs.

These chapters take you into classrooms where you will meet teachers who may be in situations similar to yours. The teachers in these chapters were created from our experiences working with K–6 teachers over the years. Although no teacher in this book represents any particular individual, they all reflect the concerns, thoughts, and actions of real teachers. Their decisions about how they have chosen to step up to the challenges they face may inspire and inform decisions you face on a daily basis.

For example, if you are a fifth-grade teacher who feels overwhelmed by the number of objectives your students are required to master by the end of the year, you might be interested in how our first-grade teacher thoughtfully plans lessons involving multiple mathematical contexts to accomplish more in her limited amount of time. Suppose you are a kindergarten teacher who has collected file cabinets full of really neat activities, but you worry that your Johnny Appleseed unit may not be addressing the important foundational mathematical concepts your children must have. Our fourth-grade teacher is grappling with similar issues. You might be interested to see how she and the math coach work together to identify what her students need to understand, to select exactly the right activity to support emerging understandings, and to create questions to uncover areas of misunderstanding that still need to be addressed.

Perhaps you are working with colleagues to plan better formative and summative assessments. Since each lesson throughout the book addresses assessment in different ways, you might be interested in analyzing the types of student responses each type of assessment may elicit. You and your colleagues may choose to adapt our teachers' assessment strategies to your specific needs. You might even have to change grade levels throughout your career. Having a range of strategies designed to teach a focused mathematics curriculum in multiple grade levels may influence the choices you make as you build your students' mathematical understandings—in whatever grade level you find yourself.

Finally, at the end of each chapter, we have provided questions that are designed to promote discussion about issues related to the strategy:

- Why would you want to apply the strategy?
- How would it impact you as a teacher?
- How does it relate to what you are already doing?
- How might you implement the strategy in your situation?

While you can think about the responses to these questions by yourself, you may also find it interesting and inspiring to discuss them with your colleagues in a professional learning community.

Now, let's investigate some ways to focus our mathematics curriculum in order to make the best use of our students' time.

Focusing the Curriculum by Building Purposeful Connections

A Model from Nature

In the Introduction, we discussed the rationale for teaching a focused mathematics curriculum in the elementary grades, using the National Council of Teachers of Mathematics *Curriculum Focal Points for Prekindergarten through Grade 8 Mathematics* (2006) as one example of a focused elementary mathematics curriculum. As we explained in the Introduction, a major goal of a focused curriculum is to build purposeful connections in order for teachers and students to be able to make sense of the myriad bits and pieces that exist in most mathematics curricula today when presented as lists of separated concepts and skills. We suggested an ecological analogy of creating *emergent structures* (complex mathematical understandings) through *curricular synergy* (the use of a focused curriculum where the whole is more than an accumulation of the parts) to illustrate a means for accomplishing this goal.

In this chapter, we use a tree as a visual model for designing a focused curriculum that highlights the emergence of a complex understanding in mathematics through the creation of purposeful connections. You can see from the following example, in which we have chosen the meaning of a fraction to be our focus, how this complex understanding emerges from a system of connected foundational experiences and understandings.

Fractions as a Focus

There are many complex understandings that begin in elementary school mathematics and are critical for further success in learning later mathematics. Many middle school teachers, responsible for teaching operations with fractions, lament the limited understanding concerning fraction concepts that their students bring with them from elementary school. It may be that students did not receive the opportunity to spend a concentrated amount of time building a strong foundation for understanding fractions as numbers, and then to continue developing this complex understanding over time. In earlier grades, students need to be led to make deliberate comparisons with, contrasts between, and connections to previously mastered whole number concepts and to form purposeful connections to other mathematical strands where fractions are useful (such as in measurement or probability).

As we think about the development of a complex understanding of fractions as an emergent structure, we must recognize the critical interactions necessary for students to build among many views of and experiences with fractions. From a variety of resources, including Fosnot and Dolk (2002), NCTM (2000), and Van de Walle (2007), we might identify the following pieces needed to support the emergence of this complex understanding.

Meanings of Fractions

- Fractions are fair shares of a whole or a set.
- Fractions describe a part-to-whole relationship.
- The denominator of a fraction can be thought of as a divisor.
- The numerator of a fraction can be thought of as a multiplier.

The Language of Fractions

- Fractions have special names that tell how many of them make up a whole. For example, four one-fourth pieces make a whole. It takes six sixths to make a whole.
- Fractions are written with one number above another, separated by a horizontal line.
- The bottom number is called the *denominator* because it names the pieces by how many there are in the whole.

- The top number is called the *numerator* because it enumerates, or counts, the pieces in the part that is being described.
- A number greater than or equal to one can be written in fraction form (an improper fraction) or as a combination of a whole number and a fraction less than one (a mixed number).

Comparing Behaviors of Fractions and Whole Numbers
- As the numerators of fractions with the same denominators increase, the fractions become greater, just like with whole numbers. For example, $\frac{3}{5}$ is greater than $\frac{2}{5}$ just as 3 is greater than 2.
- As the denominators of fractions with the same numerators increase, the fractions become smaller, which is different from how whole numbers behave. For example, $\frac{3}{5}$ is greater than $\frac{3}{7}$ although the whole number 7 is greater than the whole number 5.
- There are no other whole numbers between two consecutive whole numbers, such as 2 and 3.
- You can always find another fraction between any pair of fractions. For example, $\frac{2}{3}$ is located between $\frac{2}{4}$ and $\frac{3}{4}$.

Equivalent Fractions
- The same amount can be named by different-sized fractional parts, such as $\frac{2}{4}$ and $\frac{3}{6}$.
- Patterns can be used to identify and generate equivalent fractions, for example, by using rows or columns in a times table, by looking at ordered pairs on a Cartesian graph, or by multiplying the numerator and the denominator by the same number.
- Patterns can be used to develop algorithms for finding common denominators and to represent fractions in simplest terms.

Connections Between Fractions and Other Topics
- You can add, subtract, multiply, and divide with fractions.
- Fractions can be represented as decimals.
- Percents can be represented as fractions.
- Ratios can be represented as fractions and proportions as pairs of equivalent fractions.
- Fractions and decimals can be used to describe measurements.

- Probability is expressed as a fraction.
- Fractions are used in statistics.

A Planning Tree for Focusing Instruction

The visual model in Figure 1–1 clearly demonstrates how the growth of a structure such as the understanding of fractions leads to the development of further mathematical experiences and emerging understandings. The tree as a model for an emergent structure performs its part in an ecosystem as a complex system with connections to other complex systems.

The emergent structure—Fractions—identified as the trunk of the tree supports the development of the emerging understanding of the use of two numbers to describe a fraction, as identified in the box at the top of the tree. Components of this emerging understanding are identified in the leaves and branches of the tree. The arrows point out the purposeful connections that can be made between Fractions and other emergent structures in the *ecosystem*: Place Value, Operations, Multiplication and Division, Ratio and Proportion, Measurement, and Probability. The roots of the tree represent prerequisite understandings that support the study of fractions.

The Message in the Tree

In order to study fractions, students need to have a basic understanding of

- whole numbers and how they are used to represent quantities;
- fair shares and equal parts of a whole or a set;
- the models useful in representing fractions (geometric shapes, lines, sets); and
- the language used to describe precisely a part of a whole (e.g., three out of four equal parts).

Just as a tree's roots bring water and nutrients through the trunk to the resulting branches, so do the prerequisite understandings nurture the emergent mathematical structure—Fractions. A tree's leaves (through the process of photosynthesis) provide food for the entire organism. So, too, do the developing complex comprehensions nourish the deepening prerequisite understandings. A tree's canopy of branches and leaves provide corridors

Focused Instruction Planning Tree

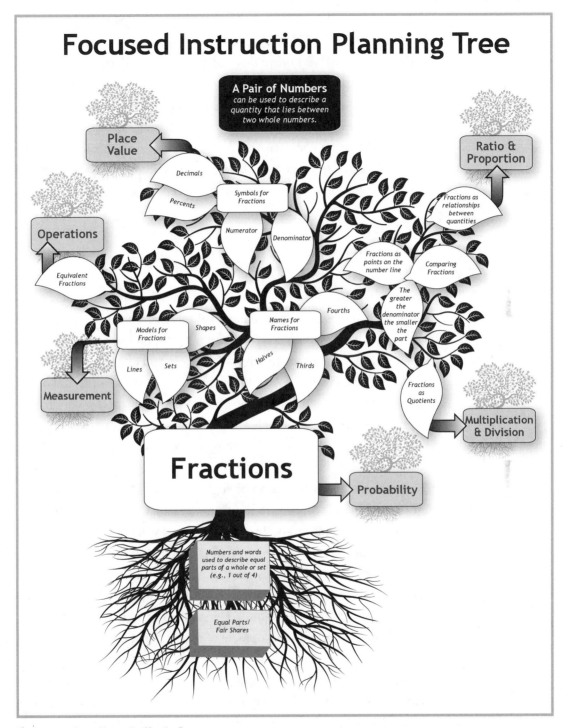

Figure 1–1 Focused Instruction Planning Tree

and pathways for the inhabitants of a forest ecosystem. So, too, do the complex understandings provide connections to other emergent structures.

The big idea of fractions offers just one example. However, from this example, we can see that when teachers use an approach in which students are led to make purposeful connections among these fraction-related concepts and between fractions and other topics in mathematics, students are able to develop the complex understanding of what fractions are before they are expected to manipulate them symbolically. The same can be said about each of the complex mathematical concepts students need to learn.

The Teacher's Role

We hope that you will be able to use this example as a guideline at the district or individual/school curriculum level to organize existing curriculum pieces into a connected whole with a few focal points at a specific grade level and with connections to the grades before and after (as in the NCTM Curriculum Focal Points). While the focus in our example is on fractions, it could just as easily be on one of the other key components for your particular grade level, such as multiplication and division or geometric shapes.

Your goal as the teacher will be to build on the concepts in the roots to provide an understanding for your focal point (the trunk) and to choose your problems and activities accordingly. What happens in the branches and the leaves will connect to the trunk and may become the focus for other lessons or grade levels. In Appendix A, you will find a blank model of a tree that you may use as a template for developing emergent structures within a focused mathematics curriculum. After identifying the desired Emerging Complex Understanding (the box at the top of the tree), use sticky notes to identify Prerequisite Understandings (the roots) and components that support the development of that understanding (the branches and leaves).

You may wish to consider engaging a team of colleagues at a campus or district level to plan a year of instruction using three or four focal points as emergent structures. You might treat each of these as a major unit of study lasting three to four weeks. Shorter units could involve connections to other content; this would provide important contexts for the ongoing application of concepts in the major units of study. It will also be important to do planning across grade levels to ensure that curricular gaps and unnecessary overlaps do not develop in clusters of grade levels.

It may be helpful to consult your library of instructional resources as you identify the components of major concepts. For example, useful discussions of ideas related to fractions appear in available resource books, including Barnett et al. (1994), Chapin and Johnson (2000), Charlesworth (2005), Clements et al. (2004), Fosnot and Dolk (2002), Lamon (1999), NCTM (2000, 2002), Payne (1990), and Van de Walle (2007). These types of books, singly or in combination, also can provide the foundation for productive lesson studies with other colleagues related to identifying the components of desired emerging understandings.

Responding to Short-Term Accountability Goals While Not Losing Sight of Long-Range Goals for Students

Based on previous experiences we have had working with school districts, we acknowledge the need to respond to the requirements of high-stakes testing. It is important, however, not to sacrifice long-term goals for short-term quick fixes. Every lesson should include important questions, observations, and products designed to seek ongoing evidence of understanding. You don't want to wait until it is too late to discover that students do not understand key mathematical concepts. Seeking this evidence should be a regular part of instruction.

Similarly, instruction need not stop in order to gauge the level of student comprehension. As teachers, we must find ways to document the results of ongoing assessment of key concepts to alleviate anxiety on the part of our administrators as well as to plan effective instruction that continues to address the ever-changing needs of all of our students. Each example lesson in the following chapters includes suggestions for this type of assessment.

Study Questions for Professional Learning Communities

1. Why might you want to build focus into your mathematics curriculum and instruction?

2. How do you see a structure like a planning tree helpful in focusing instruction?

3. What barriers do you see in using this structure to focus instruction in your existing mathematics curriculum? How might you address these barriers?

4. Look back at the Planning Tree in Figure 1–1. What is the difference between the emergent structure (Fractions) and the emerging understanding in the box at the top of the tree?

5. Select a topic at your grade in your curriculum and use the planning tree template in Appendix A to identify the major components of that topic. What is the major emergent mathematical structure (the topic box on the trunk)? What emerging understanding do you want students to develop (the box at the top of the tree)? What foundational ideas (the roots) do students need in order to work toward this understanding? What ideas do students need to develop and connect together (the branches) to develop the emerging understanding?

Designing Focused Instruction and Assessment

A Lesson Template

As we think about the mathematics learning environment in the classroom as a type of ecosystem, it becomes necessary to identify the aspects of that environment that encourage or discourage the *growth* and *adaptation* involved in learning. In this chapter, we present a template for designing lessons that contribute to an environment that supports learning in a focused curriculum. (A blank template appears in Appendix B; we will also describe the example lessons in Chapters 3 through 9 using this template.) The template includes lesson plan components that create the curricular synergy needed to promote students' abilities to understand the complex topics of focus. These lesson components include:

- plans for identifying and highlighting the purposeful connections related to the content of the lesson;
- strategies for accessing students' previous experiences and current understandings;
- questions that focus student attention on the emerging understandings; and
- techniques for orchestrating summary discussions to help students deepen and strengthen connections among their understandings and to provide the teacher with information for designing future learning experiences.

Planning for Purposeful Connections

Any well-planned lesson is based on one or more clear objectives. Consider the Fraction tree in Chapter 1. The objective(s) for a lesson should be directly related to at least one of the grade level's specific areas of focus related to that understanding (e.g., equivalent fractions). Planning for the lesson should begin with a clear description of the mathematical idea(s) addressed in the lesson (i.e., the knowledge or skill *objective* for the lesson) and how the concept(s) are important in building this and other related complex mathematical understandings (i.e., the *rationale* for the lesson). The objective and rationale are the driving forces behind the questions that you ask during the lesson and in the summary discussion at the end of the lesson. These questions enhance students' capabilities to make those purposeful connections.

A lesson that supports focused instruction must be built around a *task* that engages students physically and mentally in achieving the chosen learning objective(s). The task that the students engage in might be solving a problem, using mathematical skills to play a game, developing a mathematical strategy for winning a game, analyzing a demonstration of a particular skill, looking for a pattern, communicating a mathematical idea, or recording information mathematically. The task might be one you create from scratch or one from your textbook or other instructional resource, used as presented or adapted. It might be a task that students have never encountered before, or one that they are revisiting for a more in-depth experience. Whatever the task, it must directly address the learning objective(s) and provide opportunities for students to make purposeful connections in order to support the focused curriculum.

Thoughtful selection of *materials* for each lesson can also support a focused curriculum. Can a manipulative be incorporated into many lessons, maybe even across grade levels, to minimize the amount of time students need to become familiar with using it? Does the technology you are interested in using for a particular lesson highlight the thinking that leads to developing the complex mathematical understanding that is the focus of the lesson, or is the mathematics hidden by the technology? Is there a slightly different way you could use the technology so that the mathematics *is* highlighted? Does the literature you want to use support the purposeful connections you want students to make as a result of the lesson, or is it a great piece of literature better read at another time? Each of these planning decisions impacts how well a lesson will support focus in your mathematics instruction.

Accessing Students' Previous Experiences and Current Understandings

Because instruction in a particular area of a focused curriculum is often concentrated in a certain period of time, each task should begin with some type of *introduction* that connects the lesson to students' previous experiences and current interests and understandings. For example, you might look for a piece of literature that connects previous learning with the new lesson's objectives. In this way, a lesson focusing on selecting appropriate units of measure could be introduced with *Amelia Bedelia* (Parish 1963), in which Amelia Bedelia measures a cup of milk with a ruler (34–35).

At the same time, develop provocative questions you can ask that will get students to address their current understandings and that lead to the need for new learning. For example, "How could you use what you know about measurement to measure the strength of a magnet? For example, how close does the magnet need to be to the metal object to attract it? How heavy an object can you suspend from the magnet?"

Also think about previous experiences students have had that could be extended. For example, intuitive understandings of equally sharing food or space provide the groundwork for understanding fractions.

Determine if the task will require you to provide prerequisite or scaffolding experiences in order to prepare students for engagement. For example, it might be necessary for the class to review the use of place-value blocks and mats to represent whole numbers before they use these materials to represent decimals. These techniques for accessing students' current understandings also provide the groundwork for making connections among the concepts in a focused curriculum.

Focusing Student Attention on the Emerging Understanding

In a focused mathematics curriculum, teachers need to guide students within any given experience so they can learn what the important pieces of that experience are. Questions can be used throughout the lesson to promote productive student *engagement* in the task. You'll want to consider what questions might help students focus on the mathematics they are doing in the lesson. Remember to model the mathematical language and symbols that relate to the task and the objectives. How can you focus students' attention on important patterns and encourage them to make inferences or generalizations related to the objective? How can you help them make and test conjectures related to the objective(s) of the lesson?

You can also use questions asked and observations made during the lesson as a type of *embedded assessment* that requires very little additional instructional time. What questions do you expect students to be able to answer as they work on the task? What will you do if they are not able to answer these questions at the appropriate times? Should you adjust the task? Should you pull students aside for a quick review of a concept or skill in order to be able to continue working? As students work on the task, what do you want to look for and listen for that will provide evidence of understanding? What will you do if you do not see or hear these things?

As you design and conduct the lesson, consider also the classroom management ideas that might support productive student engagement. Should students be working individually, with partners, or in small groups? Is there a best time frame for the engagement in order to maximize learning?

Promoting Depth of Understanding

It is critical to allow students to reflect back on the thinking they've done while engaged in a rich task; this reflection deepens their understanding. A well-orchestrated *summary discussion* at the end of the lesson helps students put their new ideas together with their previous understandings into organized mathematical structures that they will be able to continue to build upon. For many students, the actual learning occurs during this summary discussion, so you want to make sure your summary discussion is rich and meaningful. In a summary discussion, students should be encouraged to do one or more of the following:

- share their problem-solving processes and solutions;
- compare solution strategies and look for different ways of approaching problems and describing solutions; and
- uncover patterns or generalizations that may serve to connect this learning experience to important complex mathematical understandings.

Teachers should also encourage students to analyze the dynamics within their individual groups, when appropriate, to improve their skills in working together. For example, how did their group handle difficulties they encountered in their tasks? How did they ensure that each group member participated and could describe how the task was being addressed? What did they think they were able to accomplish in their group that they might not have been able to accomplish individually?

Assessing Depth of Understanding

Students and teachers both need to know at all times to what extent understanding is being developed. This information is vital, because there is less time in a focused curriculum simply to repeat content. A focused curriculum requires efficient assessment procedures that provide the most information possible and take the least amount of time away from instruction.

In addition to noting the embedded assessment that goes on during the lesson, teachers can uncover evidences of understanding at the end of a lesson with *follow-up assessment*. For example, teachers may ask students to use the new mathematics they've learned by responding to a writing prompt. Similar tasks should also require them to display their depth of understanding. Students may describe a reason to use the mathematics concept(s) in the world outside of school, or they may create artwork, a song, a story, or a poem to display their depth of mathematical understanding.

Extending and Differentiating the Lesson to Engage All Students

As with any effective instructional plan, lessons designed for a focused mathematics curriculum must be able to address the different needs of students. Although some of this differentiation might come at the curricular level (e.g., core topics only versus core topics plus *extras*), there are also requirements and opportunities for differentiation at the lesson level. We believe that every student should be provided the opportunity, and whatever support is needed, to learn from engagement in each rich task.

Ideas for differentiation may include suggestions for various entry points to the task that require different levels of previous understandings or additional questions that extend students' thinking after completing the given task. Differentiation ideas can also address students' different areas of interest. For example an activity might provide a choice between a sports-related application and an arts-and-crafts type of setting. When you start out with ideas for differentiating a task, you will increase your ability to engage and challenge all of your students.

Designing Assessment for a Focused Curriculum

As you see in the lesson template in Appendix B, assessment is a major component of instruction designed for a focused curriculum. As we teach, we must continually ask ourselves the following questions:

- To what extent are my students learning the specific skills and concepts that are the goals of the lesson?
- To what extent are my students progressing toward the learning goals described in my state's curriculum standards for my grade?
- What are my students learning *beyond* the specific skills and concepts of the lesson? In other words, are they developing the connections and complex understandings that should be emerging from the curricular synergy and that form the important structures for further success in mathematics?

Each of these assessment goals can be addressed through questions and small tasks embedded within the larger lesson as well as with sets of questions or tasks presented to students following the lesson.

Embedded assessment for learning the particular goals and concepts in the lesson might simply involve looking for certain behaviors (e.g., drawing an appropriate picture to represent multiplication) or listening for appropriate use of certain vocabulary (e.g., using the correct names for polygons). Embedded assessment can be tailored to individual students as you observe their engagement in the activity by asking questions related to their specific actions. These embedded questions help students maintain focus in the curriculum because they direct all students to attend to the skills and concepts that are the focus of the lesson. They can also redirect the attention of a student who may be off-track. Finally, embedded assessment questions can be designed to highlight the connections that are crucial within a focused curriculum. For example, as students are working on adding and subtracting decimals, we should ask them questions that require them to think about how the procedures they are using relate to place value ideas.

Assessment that follows a lesson in a focused curriculum should include questions or tasks that are directly related to the specific goals of the lesson, questions designed to reflect the types of items on the state assessment related to the content of the lesson, and questions or tasks that uncover the connections students have formed between the ideas within a given lesson and other related mathematical ideas. Follow-up assessment might even include a task that requires students to connect the ideas related to several lessons, such as collecting, organizing, and analyzing a set of data to create a strategy for playing a game involving rolling two number cubes.

In general, assessment questions and tasks should address the following types of mathematical thinking as they relate to the focus of the lesson:

> ***Can students use models and mathematical symbols to explain***
> ***what they are learning?*** Ask students to represent the situation in
> a diagram, picture, chart, or table. Provide students with opportuni-
> ties to communicate their results through the use of various repre-
> sentations, including appropriate mathematical symbolism.

Can students use logical analysis to explain ideas related to the lesson? Provide students with opportunities to explain why things work the way they do. Ask students to look for the important characteristics of what is going on. Ask students to compare likenesses and differences. Ask students to identify important patterns.

Can students make inferences related to the ideas in the lesson? Encourage students to make generalizations and conjectures. Ask students to test their conjectures and transfer them to new situations.

Can students use the ideas in the lesson to design optimal strategies? Ask students to find the best or most efficient way to do something. Encourage them to use their imagination to explore many possibilities through *what if* questions. Ask them to compare and evaluate strategies.

Are students forming abstractions related to the content in the lesson? Ask students questions that focus on the lesson's mathematical purpose. Have students attempt tasks that require connections between the ideas in the lesson and prior experiences and understandings.

Using Assessment Information to Strengthen a Focused Curriculum

In addition to giving you information about what your students have learned, effective assessment can also give you information about how to strengthen your instructional design within a focused curriculum. Are students having difficulty focusing on the mathematics in the task? Perhaps there are extraneous elements of the task that can be deemphasized or eliminated. Perhaps additional components or questions need to be added to the task to highlight the mathematics being learned. Perhaps a different type of introduction to the task would provide important scaffolds for thinking about the new mathematics.

Are students coming to erroneous conclusions as a result of the learning experience? Perhaps the examples in the lesson need to be more varied.

Maybe this possibility of an erroneous conclusion needs to be addressed in the summary discussion with a specific question that calls attention to a counterexample.

Looking Forward

The detailed lessons that appear in Chapters 3 through 9 present specific applications of each of the components in the lesson template, including ideas for and possible student responses to embedded and follow-up assessment. You will read about primary teachers who have found that their students' eager questions and unbounded curiosity have led them from topic to topic in a rather disjointed way. These teachers worry that their students' mathematical understandings may have ended up haphazardly arranged and disconnected. They are now seeking ways to focus their mathematics curriculum so their students will develop a powerful network of interconnected mathematical ideas that will support the development of concepts to come.

You will also meet experienced teachers who have seen a lot of educational innovations come and go. They have learned over the years that students do not master complex mathematical understandings the first—or even second—time they encounter them in a lesson. They have decided that the only way they will be able to cover mathematics topics thoroughly is to combine them with other mathematics content to be developed at deeper and deeper levels throughout the year.

You will encounter a teacher whose grade-level curriculum has become crowded with mathematics concepts from the next grade in preparation for rigorous, high-stakes state assessments. Her goal is to work in a district-wide vertical team to balance the needs of standardized accountability measures while also respecting the developing mathematical understandings that take time to build in the primary grades. Streamlining content and focusing on mathematical core concepts (big ideas) is one technique she discovers to rise to these challenging expectations.

You will also meet a new teacher who has a lot to offer her colleagues from the college mathematics courses she has just finished taking. However, she has come to realize that she must blend these ideals with her actual experiences. And she faces many other challenges. She has chosen to work in an urban, inner-city school that is located in what some describe as an unsafe environment. Many of the students do not speak English as a first language, most are from low socioeconomic home environments, and many have parents who aren't focused on the scholastic needs of their children. For these students, especially, the focus on purposeful connections must convince them that mathematics makes sense and will serve as useful tools in their lives.

One of the teachers you will meet loves to attend conferences and workshops to collect lots of activities. She has difficulty choosing the right task for her students to do. Her math coach knows that she needs to learn to focus her attention on what her students need. Teaching a focused mathematics curriculum will require her to make decisions about what instructional materials and activities to use and what to omit.

You will also read about an experienced teacher who knows mathematics but who has taught lockstep, procedure-oriented mathematics programs her entire career. She teaches in a poor, rural community where most of the families are apathetic at best and hostile at worst. The parents of her students do not support educational goals and feel the school is a threat to them and their way of life. The spark is almost gone behind her students' eyes. They have a lot of gaps, don't see the relevance of math, and don't expect it to make sense. She knows that these kids need purposeful connections to see how all of these big ideas fit together and make sense. A focused curriculum will provide opportunities for her students to make important connections among mathematical ideas that will not only motivate them but also empower them to feel responsible for their own learning.

Last, you will meet a thoughtful teacher who teaches in a school that draws from a widely varied population—from students with parents who pout because their children did not qualify for accelerated mathematics to some students who have no parental support at all. This teacher strives to make purposeful connections to meaningful mathematics. He is not satisfied with *neatsy-cutesy* enrichment tasks designed to keep a few parents happy while other students do basic drill and practice for the rest of the time. Implementing new instructional strategies (like the use of technology to provide differentiation opportunities) requires him to revisit his thinking about instruction to maintain the focus on the mathematics his students must learn.

As a final note, although each lesson in Chapters 3 through 9 is designed for a limited span of grade levels, we encourage you to look at all of them. Each contains examples of specific approaches to designing instruction for a focused curriculum that might be useful to you, no matter which grade you teach.

Study Questions for Professional Learning Communities

1. What are the benefits of using a lesson template to focus instruction?
2. What do each of the components in the lesson template contribute to the planning of focused instruction?
3. How would using this lesson template change the way you think about planning instruction?
4. Which components are you already incorporating in your lessons?
5. Which ones are new to you? Pick one of the new components and make a plan to include it in your next lesson design. Share with another teacher how it worked.

3

Asking Targeted Questions to Focus on Foundational Understandings

A Lesson on Whole Number Concepts

I n this chapter we visit Anne, an experienced kindergarten teacher who is searching for ways to focus her mathematics curriculum so her students develop a powerful network of interconnected mathematical ideas that will support the development of concepts to come. In years past, she felt as if the children's eager questions and their unbounded curiosity led her from topic to topic in a rather disjointed way. She worries that their mathematical understandings may have ended up haphazardly arranged and disconnected. Her goal for this year is to develop classroom conversation skills that consistently target big ideas instead of allowing the children to wander off track.

Planning for Focused Instruction

Anne has decided to work with her colleagues to plan units and lessons that identify and concentrate instruction upon the foundational mathematical understandings that their kindergartners need. They have identified whole number concepts as one of the complex understandings on which they want to focus. The teachers will use the model of the tree as a way to visualize whole number concepts as a complex, purposefully organized unit of study with connections to other complex systems: Patterns, Place Value, and Operations (see Figure 3–1).

Determining the Objective and Rationale for the Lesson

The roots of their tree represent prerequisite understandings the learner brings to the study of whole numbers. The *emergent structure*—Whole Numbers—supports the development of *complex understandings* identified in the leaves and branches of the tree. The arrows point out the purposeful connections that can be made between Whole Numbers and other emergent structures in the *ecosystem*, structures such as Patterns, Place Value, and Operations. For this lesson, Anne decides to focus on composing and decomposing numbers—thinking of a whole number in terms of two parts.

Anne originally became a kindergarten teacher because she enjoys working with five- and six-year-olds. They are bright-eyed, curious, and enthusiastic. They are also wiggly and have a short attention span. She knows, too, that they tend to be teacher pleasers: they look for facial clues and body language and try to respond the way they believe their teacher expects them to respond. Lately, she has become aware that she needs to probe their thinking a little more deeply to ensure that she is not allowing an expected correct answer or behavior to mask misunderstandings. Anne wants to focus her curricular attention on what her kindergartners really need to know. She believes this will give her back the precious time she requires to figure out what each child really understands and is ready to build upon next.

Developmentally, Anne knows that when children come to her, they can generally say the counting numbers in order but may not yet connect them to finding the number of objects in a group. They are beginning to think of numbers as *adjectives* and to use them to describe actual quantities in answer to the question, "How many are there?" Some children are also able to solve simple problems such as, "Are there enough napkins for everyone in your group to have one?" Most know that each object must be counted only once as they say the counting numbers, and that they can touch the objects in any order as they count without affecting how many

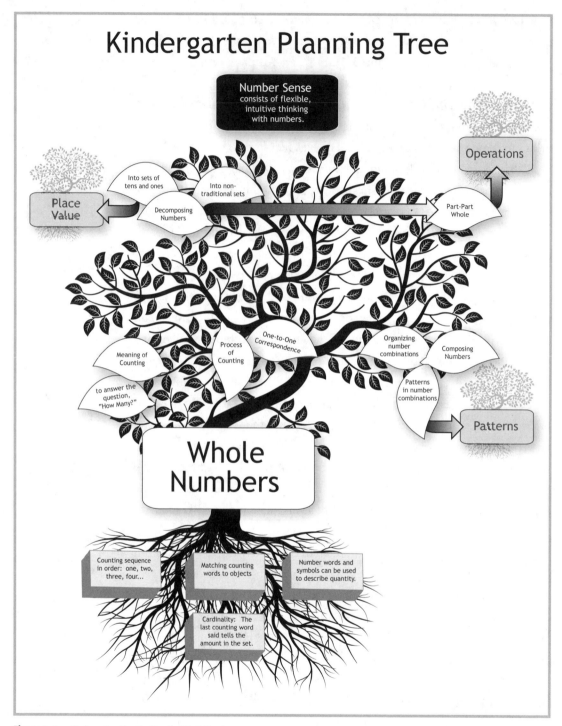

Figure 3–1   Kindergarten Planning Tree for Whole Numbers

there are. They also seem to know that the last number they say tells how many objects are in the whole group. It's not the *name* of the last object they touched as they counted.

Anne's state standards for mathematics require kindergartners to use numbers to name quantities as they use one-to-one correspondence and comparative language (such as *one more than, the same as, two less than*) to describe the number of objects in a set. They are expected to create sets of a given size and to use numerals to represent given quantities. Also, kindergarten students are expected to identify patterns and use them to make predictions and solve problems. By the end of their primary years, they are expected to flexibly compose and decompose numbers in order to solve addition and subtraction problems requiring precision, estimation, and reasonableness.

Anne and her colleagues would also like to utilize an example of a focused curriculum to guide them as they plan. They chose the following from the Curriculum Focal Points and Connections for Kindergarten (NCTM 2006, 12):

> *Number and Operations:* Representing, comparing, and ordering whole numbers and joining and separating sets   Children use numbers, including written numerals, to represent quantities and to solve quantitative problems, such as counting objects in a set, creating a set with a given number of objects, comparing and ordering sets or numerals by using both cardinal and ordinal meanings, and modeling simple joining and separating situations with objects. They choose, combine, and apply effective strategies for answering quantitative questions, including quickly recognizing the number in a small set, counting and producing sets of given sizes, counting the number in combined sets, and counting backward.

Identifying an Engaging Task, Appropriate Materials, and Questioning Strategies

In the past, Anne had planned a variety of counting activities in which she gave children a target number (such as five) and asked them to count that number of objects onto several different work mats. In order to keep the children interested, she made lots of different types of counters and scenarios available for them to choose from.

This year, because she is concentrating on providing focus in her mathematics curriculum, Anne has decided to tweak the counting stations slightly to give the children opportunities that move them beyond simple practice in counting a collection of objects. Her Whole Number Planning Tree (Figure 3–1) includes some important mathematical goals for her students. Because she wants them to know that numbers are composed of smaller numbers, she plans to ask children to see how many different ways they can count out a given quantity. She will adjust her scenarios and counters to provide ways children can think of any whole number in terms of parts (e.g., 5 as 2 and 3) as they also practice counting sets of objects to match a given quantity. In this way, Anne hopes to help her kindergartners build a more flexible understanding of numbers that will enable them to join and separate sets fluently later on. Additionally, she will probe for deeper understanding by asking questions to encourage children to organize their work, look for patterns, and use the patterns to think about finding all the different combinations of pairs of numbers that can be used to make a targeted quantity. To help her stay focused within the classroom setting, she records her thinking about her goals and objectives for the lesson (see Appendix C).

Although planning lessons in this way takes time, Anne feels it is worth it. She knows it will become easier with practice, and she believes that the example questions and observations will really help her to maintain her focus as she teaches the lesson.

Implementing the Focused Instruction

Today, Anne starts Math Time with a question for the whole class to focus attention on the quantity *five* in terms of two parts. She asks, "How many different ways can you show *five* with the fingers on both hands?"

As different children raise their hands to show five fingers, Anne asks the class to confirm that their choices are correct. She says, "Carrie is showing us three fingers on her right hand and two fingers on her left hand. Is that five?" The class agrees, and Anne invites Carrie to move to the front of the room.

Anne continues, "Does anyone have a different way to show five?" Vonica shows one finger on her right hand and four fingers on her left hand, so Anne also invites her to the front of the room. Jeff shows two fingers on his right hand and three fingers on his left hand. A discussion ensues:

STUDENT: I think Jeff's way is the same as Carrie's. If you move Jeff in front of Carrie, you can see that they have the same fingers. [The student places Jeff nose-to-nose with Carrie.] See?

STUDENT: But their fingers are on different hands! So I think they are different. Jeff, show everyone. [Jeff turns around and faces the class—still with fingers showing two and three.] See?!

ANNE: What do the rest of you think? [Several children nod vigorously.]

STUDENT: Okay. I guess Jeff is different from Carrie.

After Jeff joins the group at the front of the room, Erica raises her right fist in the air and shows five fingers on her left hand. Anne questions, "Is Erica showing us another way to make five? Let's make sure we understand what her fist means." Erica explains that her fist is showing zero fingers. The class agrees that Erica belongs at the front of the room.

Anne decides that the children are ready to think about some deeper relationships between the number combinations represented at the front of the room. She says, "I wonder if we have found all of the ways to show five with the fingers on both hands. How could we figure this out?" The children seem puzzled at first, but then Carrie suggests that Jeff's way of showing five is sort of like her way—but maybe opposite. Anne smiles at this. The class has been brainstorming examples of opposites and she is pleased to see how this is carrying over into Math Time. In years past, she might have started a discussion of other opposites. But this year, she is determined not to get distracted from the focus of her lesson—conceptualizing the quantity *five* in terms of two parts. She glances back at her plans to remind herself what comes next.

"Let's move Jeff next to Carrie to show that their ways to make five belong together. What about Vonica and Erica? Do they belong together?" Jon says they don't, but he offers to show five in a way that is the opposite of Erica's choice. To prove this, he extends all five fingers on his right hand.

To show zero, he punches the air above his head with his left fist. The class agrees that he belongs next to Erica.

Anne continues the discussion. "So have we found all the ways to make five? Should everyone up at the front of the room have a partner that shows an opposite way to make five?"

The class decides that Vonica needs a partner, and many children quickly volunteer to join her by showing four fingers on their right hand and one finger on their left. Anne asks, "So now have we found all the ways to make five? Can anyone think of a way we have missed?" The children spend several minutes comparing hands (Figure 3–2). Then the class decides that they have found all possible ways to show five with the fingers on both hands.

Next, Anne suggests that children visit centers she has set up for them to show the number five in two parts—with zero being a possible part. Children will show each new way to make five on a different work mat.

Using Embedded Assessment to Support Focused Instruction

Anne checks her plan to remind herself what she wants to know about what the children are doing and thinking. She circulates among the children working at the centers and asks questions to help students focus on the objectives of the lessons. She includes questions such as:

- How do you know you have made five? Show me how you count the objects on this work mat. Does it matter which object you touch first as you count? Are there still five counters when you start counting with this one instead of this one?
- How could you use numbers to describe how you made five?
- How do you know each work mat shows a different way to make five?
- How could you organize your work mats?
- Do you see any patterns in the different ways you made five? How could you describe those patterns?
- Do you think you have found all the ways to make five? How can you use the patterns you noticed to explain how you know you have found all the ways?

Figure 3–2 Hands Showing Different Combinations of Five

Summary Discussion to Deepen Understandings

At the end of Center Time, Anne gathers the children together to talk about their experiences. She is ready to use the questions she thought about as she planned the lesson. To begin, she asks, "What work mats and counters did you use? Tell me some of the ways you made five."

One by one, the children begin to describe ways they made five with their counters and work mats. Amanda says, "I used the toads and frogs. I started with three toads and two frogs. When we made five with our fingers, we found partners. So I knew I could make five with two toads and three frogs."

Because Anne knows that she wants to connect students' learning about numbers with later work on patterns, she asks, "Did anyone else use partners to find ways to make five? What are some of the partners you found?" Some children report that they made five with one boy and four girls on the school bus with a partner of one girl and four boys. Others explain that they used three bears on the slide and two bears in the sandbox with a partner of two bears on the slide and three bears in the sandbox.

"Did anyone use zero counters on their work mats?" Anne asks. Several children described how they used zero: five blue candles and no white candles on the birthday cake; zero red ornaments and five yellow ornaments on the tree, and so forth.

"How did you organize your work mats?" Anne continues.

"We put the partners together," Jon declares. Other heads nod as children confirm that they also used Jon's way of organizing their work.

Anne has also invited Lorenzo to bring his work mats to the circle and share how he thought about organizing them. During Center Time, as she circulated throughout the classroom, she noticed that he had organized his work in a way that did not use partnered number combinations. Lorenzo is a bit shy and at times lacks the language skills to explain his thinking, but now, with Anne's encouragement, he eagerly lays out his work mats to show the ways he found to make five. Anne prompts, "I notice you have five silver stars and zero gold stars in your first night sky, and four silver stars and one gold star in the second night sky. What do you have in your third night sky?"

"Three silver and two gold," Lorenzo responds.

"What's next?" Anne asks.

The class begins to chant with Lorenzo as they read the pattern in his stars: "Two silver and three gold; one silver and four gold; zero silver and five gold" (Figure 3–3).

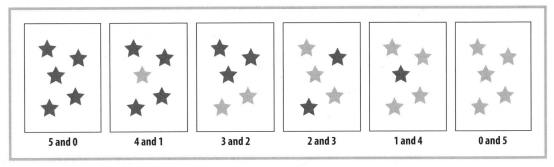

Figure 3–3 Lorenzo's Mats Showing Combinations that Make Five

Anne asks the children to describe how the number of silver stars changes from one work mat to the next.

"They get *less* each time," Katie notices.

"By how much?" Anne probes.

"By one!"

"How do the numbers of gold stars change?" Anne continues.

"They *grow* one by one!"

Anne challenges the students with a more difficult question. "How can we be sure Lorenzo has found all the ways to make five with the stars?" Some of the children look confused and are unable to describe how they know he has found them all. Others are confident as they share what they notice about the patterns and explain how the patterns help them know that there are no other ways to make five with two parts.

Examples of Follow-up Assessment

After they have had a chance to explore with the work mats, Anne pulls a few children aside individually to probe their understanding of the quantity *five* with the Hiding Assessment. First she asks a child to give her five counters. Then she hides some counters under an opaque plastic bowl, shows the rest, and asks, "How many are hiding under the bowl?" (For example, if she shows three counters and asks how many are under the bowl, the child responds that there are two.) This continues until Anne has randomly assessed all combinations of two numbers that make five.

If the student accurately and confidently tells how many counters are hidden, Anne recognizes that the child is ready to work with a greater number. She sends the student back to the center with a different target number, such as six. If the child is uncertain, makes several mistakes, or cannot immediately name the number of missing counters, Anne notes that the student needs further work with that quantity or may need to drop back to a smaller quantity, such as four.

Reflecting on the Use of Classroom Conversations

In a brief but important moment of reflection, Anne reminds herself about her goals for all of the students in her kindergarten class:

- to fluently and flexibly compose and decompose numbers at least through the quantity *five*;
- to organize their work so they can look for patterns; and
- to use the patterns to solve problems and to answer important questions about their work.

By using focused classroom conversation, Anne feels she has been able to uncover many important mathematical understandings and misunderstandings. In the past, she found herself relying on correct answers alone to indicate evidence of this understanding. In this lesson, however, she practiced asking probing questions and paying attention to the answers. Now Anne feels she is becoming more aware of whether her students can think of whole numbers in terms of parts.

Anne also recognizes that confusion on the part of some of her students is normal. She plans to give these children many other opportunities to explore whole numbers in terms of parts. In addition, she knows from the results of the Hiding Assessment that some of her students are ready to compose and decompose greater numbers. Consequently, she will do several things to meet those students' needs: change the target number for their work mats, change the number of counters they use for the extension activity ("Let's Make . . ."), and ask them to use number sentences to record the combinations they generate.

As Anne reviews what happened during the lesson, she notes that some children may be ready to investigate the patterns that emerge when the number combinations are organized in different ways. Some children are already beginning to wonder if there is a pattern in the number of ways that sets can be decomposed into two parts. *Lorenzo's Way* will become a class label for one method of organizing combinations of numbers generated on their work mats.

Finally, Anne pulls out several pieces of literature for children who are ready to decompose greater numbers and investigate their patterns. In particular, she decides to use:

- *Quack and Count* by Keith Baker (1999): decomposing the quantity seven and using number sentences to record the combinations;
- *12 Ways to Get to 11* by Eve Merriam (1993): decomposing the quantity *eleven* into two or more parts;
- *Anno's Counting House* by Mitsumasa Anno (1982): investigating the quantity *ten* in terms of two parts; and
- *Ten Flashing Fireflies* by Philemon Sturges (1995): investigating the quantity *ten* in terms of two parts.

Study Questions for Professional Learning Communities

1. Why should you have classroom conversations? What might you want to accomplish with a classroom conversation?
2. At what point within a lesson might you expect to have an important classroom conversation?
3. What information might you expect to glean from careful management of classroom conversations?
4. How do you currently use classroom conversations as a part of your lesson structure?
5. How might you change your use of classroom conversations to better focus instruction?

4

Identifying Priorities in a Focused Curriculum

A Lesson Integrating Number and Measurement Concepts

Three years ago, having taught fifth grade for five years, Theresa found herself assigned to first grade. Initially, she had to rely on her colleagues' support to understand her first graders. They helped her adjust to the children's shorter stature and even shorter attention spans. However, Theresa discovered that while her fellow teachers had extensive expertise in helping first graders develop literacy, they had little expertise in helping the children develop numeracy. A few of them confided that they really did not like math and had a difficult time finding enough for the children to do for the whole hour identified for math in their daily schedule.

In contrast, Theresa loves math. Therefore, she offered to help her team by planning the math for their grade level. They agreed with alacrity and relief.

As she plans lessons, Theresa draws from her knowledge of the struggles her fifth graders had in math. This background allows her to identify first-grade concepts that build necessary prerequisite understandings for fifth-grade concepts. As Theresa identifies these priorities, she feels she is creating ways to provide the time and attention needed for first graders to strengthen these foundational understandings.

Planning for Focused Instruction

Theresa has been attending conferences and institutes lately that have highlighted the new NCTM Curriculum Focal Points (2006). She is interested in using them to help her grade-level team identify curricular priorities. She believes that spending the time necessary to plumb the depths of important mathematics concepts will enable her first graders to develop strong foundational understandings on which to build the important key understandings yet to come. One of the Grade One Focal Points Theresa wants to develop is:

> *Number and Operations:* Developing an understanding of whole number relationships, including grouping in tens and ones   Children compare and order whole numbers (at least to 100) to develop an understanding of and solve problems involving the relative sizes of these numbers. They think of whole numbers between 10 and 100 in terms of groups of tens and ones (especially recognizing the numbers 11 to 19 as 1 group of ten and particular numbers of ones). They understand the sequential order of the counting numbers and their relative magnitudes and represent numbers on a number line. (NCTM 2006, 13)

Theresa's state mathematics standards include many of the same concepts at Grade One:

> *Number, operation, and quantitative reasoning.* The student uses whole numbers to describe and compare quantities. The student is expected to:
>
> ■ compare and order whole numbers up to 99 (less than, greater than, or equal to) using sets of concrete objects and pictorial models;
> ■ create sets of tens and ones using concrete objects to describe, compare, and order whole numbers;
> ■ identify individual coins by name and value and describe relationships among them; and
> ■ read and write numbers to 99 to describe sets of concrete objects.

Theresa has noticed that a student expectation is included in her state standards but is missing from the Focal Points: coin values and relationships. In the grand scheme of things, she decides that this expectation should not carry the same weight as the others. She will suggest to her colleagues that it should take a back seat to the focus on partitioning whole numbers into sets of tens and ones.

Determining the Objective and Rationale for the Lesson

Theresa remembers how difficult measurement concepts were for her fifth graders. They did not understand the measurement process, and they could not use measurement tools skillfully. Although measurement should have been a natural context for deepening their understanding of fractions and decimals, in reality, the use of fractions and decimals in measurements only served to compound their confusion.

From this experience, Theresa has come to realize that measurement involves concepts that are too complex to be mastered quickly. Over the primary years, students need to measure often, and teachers need to devote lots of classroom conversations to identifying attributes that can be measured and selecting appropriate units for this purpose. For Theresa's first graders, measurement will provide a reason to count and compare the results of measuring with units of different sizes. In this way, measurement will offer a rich context for developing number sense.

To begin, Theresa studies her state's standards for Grade One Measurement:

> *Measurement.* The student directly compares the attributes of length, area, weight/mass, capacity, and temperature. The student uses comparative language to solve problems and answer questions. The student selects and uses nonstandard units to describe length. The student is expected to:
>
> - estimate and measure length using nonstandard units such as paper clips or sides of color tiles;
> - compare and order two or more concrete objects according to length (from longest to shortest);
> - describe the relationship between the size of the unit and the number of units needed to measure the length of an object;
> - compare and order the area of two or more two-dimensional surfaces (from covers the most to covers the least);
> - compare and order two or more containers according to capacity (from holds the most to holds the least);

- compare and order two or more objects according to weight/mass (from heaviest to lightest); and
- compare and order two or more objects according to relative temperature (from hottest to coldest).

She also looks at the NCTM Curriculum Focal Points (2006):

> *Connections to the Focal Points—Measurement* and *Data Analysis:* Children strengthen their sense of number by solving problems involving measurements and data. Measuring by laying multiple copies of a unit end to end and then counting the units by using groups of tens and ones supports children's understanding of number lines and number relationships. Representing measurements and discrete data in picture and bar graphs involves counting and comparisons that provide another meaningful connection to number relationships. (13)

Theresa decides that the only way she and her colleagues will be able to cover the topic thoroughly is to combine it with other mathematics content and develop it at deeper and deeper levels throughout the year. This approach differs a great deal from the way she and her colleagues have taught measurement in the past. Previously, they addressed measurement in one two-week unit and then left it in order to teach the other concepts required at their grade level. Theresa hopes that focusing their efforts upon building number sense while making deliberate and consistent connections to measurement will provide her students with the opportunity they need to fully develop both.

At the conferences she has been attending, Theresa has also been introduced to different ways of visualizing the curriculum. She and her colleagues decide they like the idea of using a tree. To develop the roots for her Grade 1 Planning Tree for Whole Numbers (Figure 4–1), Theresa identifies concepts most Kindergarten students have grasped before they come to her as first graders:

- When you want to find out *how many*, you need to count.
- When you count, you point to one object at a time and say one counting word for each object.
- The last number word you say tells *how many*.

Grade 1 Planning Tree

Number Sense consists of flexible, intuitive thinking with numbers.

Operations

Place Value

Into non-traditional sets

Decomposing Numbers

Part-Part Whole

Into sets of tens and ones

One to 10 relationship

Skip counting means counting equal groups of objects.

The total remains the same no matter how objects are grouped to count.

Organizing number combinations

Composing Numbers

One to 5 relationship

One to 2 relationship

Patterns in number combinations

Whole Numbers

Counting is used to answer the question, "How many?"

The arrangement of the objects does not affect the total.

Objects being counted can be touched in any order without changing the total.

Figure 4–1   Grade 1 Planning Tree for Whole Numbers

- It doesn't matter which object you point to first or last. The order in which objects are counted does not change how many there are.

The branches of Theresa's number tree include a complex network of interconnected number concepts, each of which contribute to the understanding of place value and operations:

- You can think of a whole in terms of its parts.
- It doesn't matter how you group a set of objects to count them. The total remains the same.
- Skip counting means counting equal groups of objects.
- Numbers can be partitioned into standard sets of tens and ones (37 is 3 tens and 7 ones).
- Numbers can be partitioned into nonstandard sets of tens and ones (37 is 2 tens and 17 ones; 37 is 1 ten and 27 ones).

To create the Grade 1 Planning Tree for Length (Figure 4–2), Theresa relies on lots of reading and her memories of the fifth-grade students she taught over the years. She remembers teaching them that the *process* of measuring is the same no matter which attribute you are measuring. She recalls the components of the measurement process as:

- identifying the attribute being measured (such as *length*);
- selecting an appropriate unit (such as the length of a toothpick);
- making an estimate (such as about how many toothpicks it will take to equal the width of a desk);
- comparing the unit to the object being measured (such as carefully laying the toothpicks end-to-end with no gaps or overlaps); and
- reporting the number of units (such as, "the desk is 24 toothpicks wide").

Kindergartners understand length based on experiences with direct comparisons, such as, "My crayon is shorter than my pencil. The table is taller than the stool. The doorway is wider than the chair." Therefore, kindergartners can be expected to compare and order objects directly according to length. It is up to first graders to quantify objects according to units of length.

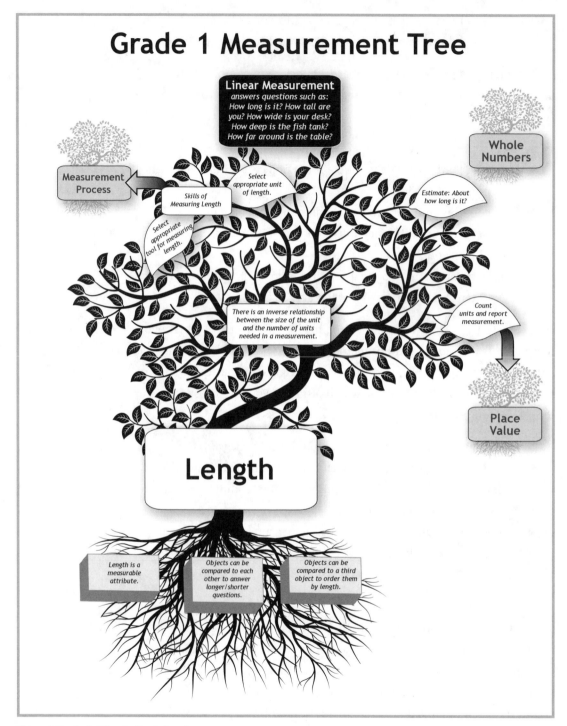

Figure 4–2 Grade 1 Planning Tree for Length

As Figure 4–2 shows, Theresa includes the following in the branches of her tree:

- We use linear measurement to answer questions such as:
  - How long is it?
  - How tall are you?
  - How wide is your desk?
  - How deep is the fish tank?
  - How far around is the table?
- Skills of Measuring Length
  - Select appropriate tools for measuring length.
  - Select appropriate unit of length.
  - Estimate: About how long is it?
  - Count units and report measurement.
- There is an inverse relationship between the length of the unit and the number of units needed in a measurement; in other words, the longer the unit used, the fewer the number of units needed in the measurement, and the shorter the unit used, the greater the number of units needed in the measurement.

Counting is still an important skill at the first-grade level. Theresa understands the importance of helping her students move beyond one-to-one correspondence to one-to-group correspondence in which they utilize the skip-counting patterns to count equal groups of objects. She decides that her lesson must give her students lots of opportunities to count objects grouped in a variety of ways (by twos, fives, and tens). A logical context for counting seems to be measuring length using a variety of nonstandard units. Theresa identifies the following objectives for her lesson:

- Length is an attribute that can be measured.
- Units of length must be uniform in size and must have the attribute of length.
- There is an inverse relationship between the length of a unit and the number needed to equal the length being measured.
- Skill must be used to compare units of length to the length being measured—no gaps, no overlaps.

- Estimation can be used to predict about how many units of length it will take to equal an object or distance.
- Objects can be counted using a variety of different-sized groups without changing the total number of objects.
- To be skip-counted, groups must contain the same number of objects.
- Grouping by tens and ones is directly related to the notation used to record the number of objects.

Identifying an Engaging Task, Appropriate Materials, and Questioning Strategies

Theresa wants to use a whole-group experience to introduce her lesson and give students an opportunity to estimate and count to verify their measurement. She will then ask children to work with a partner to investigate how changing the size of their unit of length will change their measurement. She knows that this will take several days, so she decides to plan a variety of Estimation Stations for students to visit while they wait for their turn.

From the reading she has done, Theresa knows that estimation is not easy for young learners. They don't understand what an estimate is or what the word *about* implies. She also knows that estimation is a critical component of *number sense*—often defined as flexible, intuitive ideas about numbers (Van de Walle 2007). Theresa's task cards and classroom questions will make use of language such as, "Is the length more or less than _____? Do you think it is closer to _____ or to _____? About how wide is the _____?"

At each Estimation Station, students will record an estimate by choosing "More than _____" or "Less than _____"; group units to count them; and record the actual measurement. Students will then estimate using a different object or unit. The situations at the Estimation Stations will include:

- How many lentils will fill the lid? How many kernels of popcorn will fill the lid?
- How many snap cubes will fill the jar? How many centimeter cubes will fill the jar?

- Using the balance scale, how many cubes will balance the scissors? How many paper clips will balance the scissors?
- How many tiles will cover the shape? How many centimeter cubes will cover the shape?
- How many pennies will fill the medicine bottle? How many lima beans will fill the medicine bottle?
- How many snap cubes can you grab with one hand? How many pinto beans can you grab with one hand?

Theresa records her planning for the lesson (see Appendix D) as a reminder of her expectations for her students.

Implementing the Focused Instruction

Theresa gathers her students together near the chalkboard at the front of the room and asks, "About how many craft sticks do you think it will take to equal the length of the chalk tray? Do you think it will be more than 25? Or less than 25?"

These first graders are used to thinking about numbers of objects inside a container. They are also familiar with craft sticks. In kindergarten, they used the sticks to count the number of days they had been in school. But the children have never been asked to use craft sticks to think about length.

Theresa allows a brief silence to give them time to think. Then she gives the children sticky notes on which to write their names. Depending on their guess, the children place the notes rather haphazardly on a piece of chart paper that Theresa has divided in half and labeled, "More than 25" and "Less than 25." The sticky notes seem to be evenly divided between the two halves of the chart.

"Hmmmmm!" Theresa comments. "Which guess has the most? Which has the least?" When no one answers, Theresa asks, "How could we figure this out?" Finally, Damon suggests that they line up the sticky notes to see which line is longer. A few classmates help him do this, and the class discovers that the "More than 25" side of the chart has three more sticky notes than the "Less than 25" side of the chart.

"Tell you what," Theresa says. "I'll line up ten craft sticks in the chalk tray and we'll see if that helps us with our guesses."

"You know," Hammond remarks. "This doesn't help *me* at all. I'd like to know where the *half mark* on the chalk tray is."

"How could we do this?" asks Theresa.

Hammond rushes to the supply table and brings back a ball of twine. He and a classmate cut a piece of twine the same length as the chalk tray. As the class watches, Hammond folds the piece of twine in half, lays it back in the chalk tray, and marks where it ends with chalk on the board. The class notices that the ten sticks do not reach the half mark.

"Does anyone want to change where they put their guesses on our chart?" Theresa challenges.

A few of the children hop up to move their sticky notes from the "Less than 25" side of the chart. When Theresa asks them to explain why, one child replies, "Because Rachel moved hers."

Rachel seems thoughtful, but she is not ready to describe her reasoning. She says, "I just think it's more than 25 now."

Theresa decides it is time to finish laying craft sticks in the chalk tray until they are close to the end. She invites Eric and James to do this while the other children watch. She asks the class, "What do you notice about how Eric and James are putting the sticks in the chalk tray? Are they being careful where they put them?" Damon suggests that the sticks should just touch, and Eric double-checks their work.

As the boys get close to the end of the chalk tray, Theresa asks, "Do they fit exactly?" They do not. There seems to be room for part of a craft stick, but not a whole one. "How shall we handle this?" she asks the class. Heads turn to Hammond, master of *half*!

"Well," Hammond says. "Let's see how much of a stick sticks out at the end of the chalk tray."

"We can break it off," suggests James.

Theresa turns back to Hammond. "What do you suggest, Hammond?"

"Let's just make a mark on the last stick to show where it matches the end of the chalk tray." The class seems satisfied with Hammond's solution.

Theresa notices that some of the students are starting to fidget, but she wants to bring closure to this part of the lesson before they leave for music and gym. She asks one of the fidgeting children to come count the craft sticks and another to write the number of craft sticks on the chalkboard. She continues, "So what did we find out? Did it take more than 25 or less than 25 craft sticks to equal the length of the chalk tray?"

"It took 27 and a part of another stick!" the class choruses. "That's *more* than 25!"

Theresa's planning period occurs while her students are in music and gym. As she reflects over her lesson so far, she realizes that because she is following her planning tree and her lesson plan, with its list of prepared questions, she has been able to resist teaching an impromptu lesson on finding *half.* Hammond's solution has surprised her, but it seems quite sufficient for the moment.

At the same time, Theresa worries that her need to move on did not give her the opportunity to probe Rachel's thinking and discuss how it might be related to her evolving number sense. Theresa decides to take the first opportunity available to have a conversation with Rachel. Her goal of focusing her instruction also gives her a clear plan for the short time she will have with her students when they return from music and gym. She wants to concentrate on grouping the craft sticks to count them and comparing the totals to the total they got when they counted the sticks by ones. The students return, and the discussion begins.

THERESA: Before we left for music and gym we counted the craft sticks that are lined up in the chalk tray. How many did we count?

STUDENT: We counted 27 sticks and part of another one.

THERESA: Let's look at the last stick to see where we marked it. Is most of the stick *on* the chalk tray, or *off* the chalk tray?

STUDENT: Most of the stick is *on* the chalk tray.

THERESA: Then let's include that stick in our total. We need to rewrite our total to make it 28. If we count the sticks in groups of five, do you think we will get the same total?

STUDENT: I think we'll get more because fives are more than ones.

STUDENT: I think it'll be the same.

THERESA: What happens when we run out of groups of five to count?

STUDENT: When we run out of fives, we have to count by ones.

STUDENT: We counted 5, 10, 15, 20, 25, 26, 27, 28. Hey! We still have 28!

THERESA: Now suppose we group the sticks in sets of two. What do you think will happen? What about sets of ten? How many groups of ten can you make? How many extras? What is our total?

STUDENT: I think if we count by tens, we'll get more. But by twos, we should get less.

STUDENT: I think it'll be the same. It doesn't matter how we count them!

THERESA: [Referring to the total number of craft sticks posted where all could see it] Did the number change when we grouped the sticks in different ways to count them? How can you explain this? [Several children seem positive that the number does not change—no matter how they are grouped. Others are just as positive that counting by a bigger group will result in a bigger number. Still others are not sure.]

THERESA: Let's look at the number we wrote. What did we write in the tens place? What about the ones place? Which way of grouping your sticks gave us results that are closest to the actual number we wrote to show the total?

STUDENT: We got five groups of five sticks and three extras.

STUDENT: When we grouped by tens, we got two groups and eight extras. Hey! That's just what we wrote—2 tens and 8—28!

Theresa gives pairs of students one craft stick and some toothpicks and asks them to estimate the number of toothpicks it will take to equal the length of the chalkboard. "Talk with your partner and then write your estimate in crayon on a sticky note. Post your estimates on the class graph of toothpick estimates." Theresa then introduces the Estimation Stations. She explains how the partners will work with them while they wait for their turn to measure the chalk tray with toothpicks. Pairs of students begin to approach the chalkboard to use toothpicks to verify their estimates.

Using Embedded Assessment to Support Focused Instruction

As students work, Theresa circulates to assess their number and measurement sense. She pays particular attention to how students are using the toothpicks to measure the chalk tray. Are they laying them carefully end-to-end with no gaps and no overlaps?

Theresa asks students first to count the toothpicks by ones and record the total. Then she encourages them to put the toothpicks in equal groups (such as twos, fives, or tens) to count them again. Next, she invites them to compare their new totals with the results they got when they counted their toothpicks by ones. Her number sense assessment questions include:

- Do you think the total will change when you group the toothpicks by twos [fives, tens]? Why or why not?
- What will you do when you run out of groups of twos [fives, tens] to count?

Theresa also assesses student understanding by observing and listening.

- Do students know the skip-counting sequence patterns for twos, fives, and tens?
- Do they use the skip-counting sequence to count equal groups of toothpicks?
- Do they continue to count by twos, fives, or tens when they run out of equal groups to count? Or do they switch to counting by ones?

Summary Discussion to Deepen Understandings

When all of the students have completed their toothpick measuring task and most of the Estimation Stations, Theresa gathers them around her to ask the important questions she has developed. Her questions focus first on the context she is using for developing number sense: Measurement and Data.

THERESA: How did you guess the number of toothpicks it would take to equal the chalk tray? Did you just pull a number out of the air? Or did you use some information to help you?

STUDENT: We thought it would take more than the craft sticks, so we guessed a bigger number.

STUDENT: We guessed less because toothpicks are smaller than craft sticks.

STUDENT: When we put the toothpicks next to our craft stick, we saw it took almost three toothpicks to match it. So we guessed a really big number.

THERESA : How should we organize your toothpick guesses? What do you notice about your guesses?

STUDENT: We could put the guesses into piles for "more than" and "less than." All we have to do is pick a number like we did before.

STUDENT: I think we should put them in order from smallest number to biggest number.

STUDENT: Hey, our row of guesses looks sort of like a number line. But it doesn't start until twelve.

STUDENT: It looks like a bunch of people guessed numbers in the middle of the row.

THERESA: How many toothpicks did it take to equal the chalk tray? Did everyone come up with the same total? How can you explain this?

STUDENT: We lost our paper we wrote it on, but we remember it took a *lot*!

STUDENT: It took us a long time to count them, and we kept starting over. But we got 92.

STUDENT: We got 89.

STUDENT: We got 96.

STUDENT: We got 87.

STUDENT: How come we got different numbers? Maybe we weren't careful. Toothpicks sure are little. Maybe we got in a hurry. We dropped ours and had to start counting again.

STUDENT: So how long is the chalk tray? We should do it again and be more careful.

Theresa's next set of questions focuses on grouping objects to count them, the relationship between the groups of tens and ones to the numeral, and the inverse relationship between the length of the unit and the number of units needed to measure length.

THERESA: How did you group your toothpicks to count them? When you counted your toothpicks in groups, did the total change? How can you explain this?

STUDENT: We used rubber bands to tie together groups of five toothpicks. Then we counted by fives. We still got 87.

STUDENT: We counted by twos and kept getting mixed up. So we
switched to tens. And we still got 92.

STUDENT: We still got 89. We counted by fives.

THERESA: What number did you write to show the total number of
toothpicks that matched the chalk tray? What number did you write
in the tens place? What number did you write in the ones place?

STUDENT: We wrote 94. 9 tens and 4 ones.

STUDENT: When we counted by tens, it matched what we wrote.

THERESA: When we used craft sticks to measure the length of the chalk
tray, how many did it take? When you used toothpicks, did you get
a higher number or a lower number? How can you explain this?

STUDENT: We got 28 craft sticks and 82 toothpicks. So the numbers are
the same. But it took a lot longer to count the toothpicks.

STUDENT: Hey! The numbers are NOT the same! They're backward.
82 is more than 28.

STUDENT: Toothpicks are shorter than craft sticks. So we had to use more.

Theresa's final set of questions focuses on what makes a good unit of
length. However, the lesson has become too long, so she decides to save
them for another day.

Examples of Follow-up Assessment

For additional assessment, Theresa will ask students to generate questions
about length, such as "How tall am I?" "How far is my desk from the classroom door?" "How wide is my desk?" "How long is the bookcase?" She
will use these questions to create a Length Chart, and then invite students
to select one of the questions to answer. As they work, students will need to
do the following:

- Estimate the number of craft sticks that will equal the length being
  measured (More than _____? or Less than _____?).
- Record the estimate.
- Line up craft sticks until they equal the length being measured.

- Group the craft sticks by tens and extras to record the actual measurement.
- Estimate the number of toothpicks that will equal the same length.
- Record the estimate.
- Line up toothpicks until they equal the length being measured.
- Group the toothpicks by tens and extras to record the actual measurement.
- Talk about what they discovered.

If students finish early or need an additional challenge, Theresa will provide a more complex measurement task such as the following:

Choose a box of supplies, such as ribbon, twine, masking tape, linking cubes, paper clips, drinking straws, coffee stirrers, craft sticks, toothpicks, or clothespins. Then invent a way to measure something that is not straight, such as around the top of a trash can or the circumference of a watermelon, large pumpkin, or round table. Try out your method and describe how well you think it worked.

Reflecting on Identifying Curricular Priorities

After school, Theresa reflects on her lesson. She is interested in the fact that some of her students do not yet conserve numbers. They believe that grouping objects in different ways to count them will result in a different total. Other students think the question is ridiculous because they are so certain that it doesn't matter how they group objects to count them. These students recognize that they will always come up with the same quantity. Still, others are not sure. Those students need more time and more experiences counting the same group of objects using different groupings.

Theresa also makes notes about which of her students clearly understand the inverse relationship between the length of the unit and the number it takes to equal the length of the chalk tray. Although the number of toothpicks varied, all of her students counted quite a few more toothpicks than craft sticks. And one group was able to describe their reasoning by saying, "It takes almost three toothpicks to equal one craft stick, so we guessed a really big number." What this pair seems to lack is number sense—the result of tripling a number.

Theresa now realizes that separately addressing students' number and measurement expectations would not have provided the context to build the important foundation on which to construct the mathematical understandings yet to come. She also knows that identifying and focusing on these curricular priorities will buy the time necessary to plumb the depths of these important mathematical concepts. She feels sure that measurement will continue to provide the rich source her first graders need in order to estimate, count, and verify that grouping the same objects in different ways to count them will not affect the total.

Study Questions for Professional Learning Communities

1. What are the benefits and drawbacks of identifying priorities in grade levels?
2. In the NCTM Focal Points, there is no Focal Point about data until grade 8. How can teachers in earlier grades develop some of the prerequisites needed to prepare students for the focus on data in grade 8?
3. How could you convince your principal that identifying curricular priorities and integrating student expectations is an efficient and effective way of teaching mathematics?
4. Review your grade level's mathematics curriculum, and select two important ideas that would benefit from being integrated. Explain your reasoning as you would in the Rationale and Objectives section in the Lesson Template.
5. During the activity and the summary discussion, what kinds of questions could you ask students in order to help them integrate these ideas?

5

Balancing Accountability and Sense Making in a Focused Curriculum

A Lesson on Place Value

Meet Dorothy, whose friends call her Dot. She has been a teacher for thirty-plus years—including more than twenty in the same second-grade classroom. Still, anyone who might expect Dot to be ready to slow down and rest on her laurels would be wrong. Every year at the end of the school year, Dot tearfully waves good-bye to her current crop of second graders, takes down her bulletin boards, reorganizes her centers and tubs of manipulatives, and closes her classroom door for the summer. The first of July finds her in the teacher outlet buying nametags, class incentive charts, new sets of stickers—eagerly talking about the latest workshop she has attended and how much she is looking forward to her next group of students!

Dot has seen a lot of educational innovations come and go. She has also seen the neighborhood around her campus change. When she started teaching, the neighborhood was filled with college professors and young professionals. Now most of them live in the newer neighborhoods at the edge of town. In years past, Dot recalls, anxious parents delivered their children to the door on the first day of school, proudly confiding that they had already memorized the times tables and were chomping at the bit to master the long division algorithm. Lately, she has noticed an increasing number of moms and dads who are trying to hold down two or three jobs at the same time they are juggling the challenges of single parenthood. While their children are no less precious to them, these families rarely have time to worry about multiplication tables. They are more concerned with putting food on the table and keeping the family car patched together so they can get to all of their jobs.

At the same time, Dot has noticed that the expectations for her grade level have changed rather dramatically. In her state, third grade is the first year of rigorous standardized testing in both reading and math. As a result, the second-grade math curriculum has become crowded with more and more third-grade content while her district attempts to ready its students for high-stakes assessment. Dot's biggest concern is how to balance her responsibilities to the accountability requirements with her knowledge of what second graders need to understand in order to be able to make sense of the mathematics.

Planning for Focused Instruction

Dot knows that her students are not miniature third graders. Last year, her principal encouraged her to work in a district-wide vertical team to balance the needs of standardized accountability measures while also respecting the developing mathematical understandings that take time to build in the primary grades. This year she has decided to focus her attention on thoroughly developing her students' understanding of place value. She feels that this understanding is key to providing the support needed for mathematical content in third grade and beyond. The vertical team has been studying the NCTM Curriculum Focal Points and has discovered that the Focal Points seem to parallel pretty closely their own state's math standards. Dot is interested in using the following Focal Point to plan her math content for next year:

> *Number and Operations:* Developing an understanding of the base-ten numeration system and place-value concepts Children develop an understanding of the base-ten numeration system and place-value concepts (at least to 1000). Their understanding of base-ten numeration includes ideas of counting in units and multiples of hundreds, tens, and

ones, as well as a grasp of number relationships, which they demonstrate in a variety of ways, including comparing and ordering numbers. They understand multidigit numbers in terms of place value, recognizing that place-value notation is a shorthand for the sums of multiples of powers of 10 (e.g., 853, as 8 hundreds + 5 tens + 3 ones). (NCTM 2006, 14)

The state standards on place value that Dot and her colleagues are responsible for teaching are as follows:

2.1 Number, operation, and quantitative reasoning. The student understands how place value is used to represent whole numbers. The student is expected to:

- use concrete models of hundreds, tens, and ones to represent a given whole number (up to 999) in various ways;
- use place value to read, write, and describe the value of whole numbers to 999; and
- use place value to compare/order whole numbers to 999 and record the comparisons using numbers and symbols (<, =, >).

2.5 Patterns, relationships, and algebraic thinking. The student uses patterns in numbers and operations. The student is expected to:

- use patterns in place value to compare and order whole numbers through 999.

Dot's vertical team has noticed that the NCTM Curriculum Focal Points mention a couple of student expectations that are not included specifically in their state standards, such as (a) counting units and multiples of tens and hundreds and (b) the recognition that place-value notation is a shorthand for the sums of multiples of powers of ten. Otherwise, the list of student expectations in her state standards parallels very closely both the spirit and the specifics in the NCTM Curriculum Focal Points. Dot has decided that if her students develop a thorough understanding of place value, they will show this by exhibiting the behaviors listed in both the NCTM Curriculum Focal Points and her state standards. She does not consider the examples mentioned in the NCTM publication as additional burdens.

On Dot's campus, there are four sections of second grade. She feels fortunate that, although each teacher teaches all subjects, she is able to partner with Jen—who has been teaching second grade for three years—to plan all of the mathematics and science for her grade level. Throughout the summer, Dot and Jen have met over coffee to plan their year in mathematics. Dot has brought Jen up to date with what she has learned with her vertical team, and Jen agrees that their focus should be the development of place value concepts.

Determining the Objective and Rationale for the Lesson

This morning, they have decided to create a Place Value Tree. For a few moments, they both sit and stare at the empty roots and branches. The only thing they have written down is "Place Value" on the trunk of the tree! Taking a deep breath, Dot suggests that they start by brainstorming a list of skills and understandings they *hope* their new second graders will bring to their study of place value. Dot will write each of these on a sticky note and eventually place them in the roots of their tree.

"Well," Jen begins. "Most of my second graders are able to count objects in a set. But when do they learn to skip count by tens? I think that will be important for understanding tens and ones." After quickly checking to see what their state standards require of first graders, they learn that they are expected to skip count by twos, fives, and tens. "You know," Jen continues, "my second graders seem to know the skip-counting words, but I have not been sure they all understand that they are really counting equal groups of objects as they recite the words."

Dot smiles as she remembers a conversation she had with her five-year-old grandson, Ian, which she shares now with Jen:

> One morning, Ian asked me how old I was. I decided—as usual—to turn my answer into a math lesson. I said, "If you will close your eyes, Ian, I will count out enough pennies to show how old I am—one penny for each year."
>
> When Ian opened his eyes, he said, "Man! That's a LOT of pennies! How are we ever going to count them all? It will take forever!!" I suggested that we group them so counting would be easier. We got busy and made six piles of ten pennies. There were three left over.
>
> "How should we count these groups, Ian?" I asked.
>
> "By *tens*!" he shouted. Then Ian began counting flawlessly by tens—until he got to the three extra pennies. At that point, he continued to count by tens: "Seventy, eighty, ninety! Grandmommy, are you ninety years old?!"

Dot and Jen decide that using skip counting to count equal groups of objects belongs in the roots of their tree along with One-to-One Correspondence. They decide to call it *One-to-Group Correspondence.*

Dot remarks that she has also noticed over the years that most of her second graders have Conservation of Number. They seem to understand that if no counters are added or taken away from a set, it doesn't matter how the set is arranged or rearranged. The total does not change. However, some of her students are not really sure that when they are counting the same set of objects grouped in different ways—such as by twos or fives—the total remains the same. Since that idea is an important prerequisite understanding for partitioning numbers into tens and ones, they decide to add that to the roots of their tree.

Heartened by their progress, they decide to think about what the branches of the Place Value Tree should include. Jen suggests that they might want to add something about different kinds of objects that can be used to represent numbers. She remembers a teacher's workshop last year in which the participants investigated strengths and weaknesses of different models and discussed how important good models are to support students' understanding of abstract concepts such as place value.

Dot remembers an article by Sharon Ross (1989) from an old *Arithmetic Teacher* she ran across the other day and goes to her file cabinet to retrieve it. The article mentions four properties that characterize our number system:

- *Positional property*: The quantities represented by individual digits are determined by the position they hold in the numeral.

- *Base-ten property*: The values of the positions increase in powers of ten from right to left.

- *Multiplicative property*: The value of an individual digit is found by multiplying the face value of the digit by the value assigned to its position.

- *Additive property*: The quantity represented by the whole numeral is the sum of the values represented by the individual digits. (47)

(List above used with permission of NCTM, from *Arithmetic Teacher*, 36(6), 1989; permission conveyed through Copyright Clearance Center, Inc.)

When Jen recovers from the fact that the article is almost as old as she is, they both agree that these properties belong in the branches of their tree (see Figure 5–1).

It takes Dot and Jen several visits over the summer to feel that their Place Value Tree is good enough to provide the focus they need. They decide that they can fill in some holes as they discover them throughout the year. At this point, they feel ready to plan some lessons.

Identifying an Engaging Task, Appropriate Materials, and Questioning Strategies

Dot remembers a game called *100 or Bust!* that she has been using for years (Schielack and Chancellor 1995). In this game, students roll a die seven times, each time placing the rolled digit in either the ones or tens place on a recording chart to generate a final sum as close to 100 as possible without going over. Students also record the amount chosen for each roll by placing the appropriate base-ten blocks on a hundred grid, and they keep a running total by entering each addend on a calculator. If students work in groups of three, one student can roll the die and record the selected value on the chart, the second student can place the corresponding base-ten blocks on the hundred grid, and the third student can record using the calculator. Imagine that a student rolls a 3. Figure 5–2 illustrates the models showing the team's decision for their first roll.

Dot and Jen feel that this game will be perfect to address several different ideas in the branches of their Place Value Tree:

- Numbers can be represented using a variety of models (base-ten blocks, calculators, a chart).
- Standard partitioning: Numbers can be partitioned into standard groups (tens and ones).
- Positional property
- Base-ten property

Dot and Jen are also concerned that their focus on developing place-value concepts will prevent them from ensuring that all of their state math standards for second grade are taught throughout the year. They know that

Grade 2 Planning Tree

Place Value Notation
allows us to represent numbers of any size using only ten digits.

"Bundleable" objects: sticks grouped into tens and extras

Models for representing numbers

Proportional objects: base-ten blocks

Non-Proportional Objects: money, colored chips

Base-Ten Property

Multiplicative Property

Additive Property

Flexible Partioning into hundreds, tens, and ones

Positional Property

One hundred as a unit

Ten as a unit

Operations

Place Value

One-to-Group Correspondence: Skip counting equal groups of objects

Part Whole Reasoning: Numbers are made up of smaller numbers.

Numbers as Adjectives: Numbers used to describe groups of objects

Conservation of Number: The total does not change regardless of how objects are arranged or grouped.

One-to-One Correspondence: Counting is used to answer the question, "How many?"

Figure 5–1   Grade 2 Planning Tree for Place Value

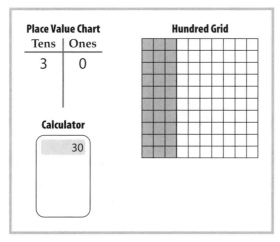

Figure 5–2 Modeling the Decision for the First Roll in *100 or Bust!*

Figure 5–3 Modeling on the 0–100 Number Line

measurement is a real challenge for students in second grade and beyond. Therefore, they decide to use measurement wherever possible to provide a context for teaching a variety of math concepts. At this point, Jen comes up with a great idea: "Hey, we could add a fourth group member to the *100 or Bust!* game to provide a connection to linear measurement." This person will have a zero to one hundred number line (represented by a meter stick) on which to plot each of the seven rolls of the die with a green triangle from pattern blocks (see Figure 5–3).

Implementing the Focused Instruction

Shortly after her new group of second graders arrive to begin the school year, Dot decides it is time to teach her Place Value Lesson involving the game *100 or Bust!* (see the full lesson plan in Appendix E). She begins by asking her students a provocative question as a warm-up in order to pre-assess their understanding of the positional and base-ten properties of place value. She is also interested in how her second graders are progressing in their ability to work productively as part of a problem-solving team.

She organizes her class into groups of four and asks, "What if seven people have a total of exactly 100 dollars? Each person has either all one-dollar bills or all ten-dollar bills. How much money could each person have?"

Her students eagerly begin using play money to act out the situation. Dot immediately sees that this is a much more involved problem than she had anticipated. As she circulates, she notices that some groups have randomly dealt out bills and counted them up. Others have tried to develop some sort of system. Still others are not able to figure out how much money they have altogether after dealing it out randomly. She also writes notes to herself about which students are able to think of ten as a unit and add multiples of ten in their heads. Other students, she notes, are still counting by ones and are a little shaky about shifting between tens and ones to find their totals.

After about fifteen minutes, Dot interrupts them to ask about their progress.

> DOT: Has any group found a solution? How did you figure it out?
>
> STUDENT: We started by making seven piles and giving everyone ten dollars. But that was only seventy dollars and we needed a hundred. So then we gave everyone twenty dollars and that didn't work because we got to one hundred dollars before all seven people got money. We decided to give four people twenty dollars, one person ten dollars, and two people five dollars. And that worked.
>
> DOT: Is that the only solution? Does it match everyone else's solution?
>
> STUDENT: *Hey!* Ours is different! One person could have forty dollars and another could have thirty dollars which is seventy dollars. One person could have ten dollars and the other four people could have five dollars each.
>
> STUDENT: We found fifty dollars and forty dollars for two people. That makes ninety dollars. Then the other five people could have two dollars each. Is that one hundred dollars? Let's make sure.

STUDENT: We found some things that *don't* work! If six people have two dollars each, that's only twelve dollars. (We counted by *two*s!) Then the person who is left has to have both tens and ones and that's against the rules.

Dot suggests to her class that they put this problem in a center and spend some time working on it. She will come up with a way for them to record their solutions (Figures E–1 and E–2) so they can later look for patterns.

Since there is about thirty minutes left before the students have to leave for music, Dot decides to go ahead and introduce the game *100 or Bust!* She explains that this game is played in groups of four. The group will roll the die exactly seven times. They will record each digit they roll in either the ones or the tens column to try to make a sum that is less than or equal to 100. Each member of the group has a specific responsibility:

- The first student rolls the die and writes each of the resulting digits in the correct column on a place-value chart.
- The second student uses base-ten blocks to show the amounts on the hundred grid as they are written on the chart.
- The third student uses the green triangle to point to the accumulating total on the number line represented by the meter stick.
- The fourth student uses the calculator to keep a running total by adding the amount of each roll of the die.

Dot plays an example game on the overhead projector, using the recording sheet to demonstrate each student's responsibility (see Figures E–3 and E–4).

She allows time for each group to play one game. The next day, the students quickly review what they did, discuss their questions, and play three more games.

Using Embedded Assessment to Support Focused Instruction

As they work, Dot circulates to ask the questions she and Jen developed in their lesson planning. She carries a clipboard and sticky notes to jot down observations.

DOT: What information does the place-value chart give you that the other three don't?

STUDENT: It helps you know which turn you are on and how many turns you have left.

DOT: What do the base-ten blocks on the hundred grid show that the calculator and place-value chart don't?

STUDENT: They show you how close you are to going *bust*!

STUDENT: It helps you decide whether to make your roll tens or ones by looking at how much you have left to go.

DOT: What does the number line help you do?

STUDENT: It also helps you know your total.

STUDENT: It helps you know how far you have to go to reach one hundred.

DOT: What does the calculator help you do?

STUDENT: It keeps track of your total.

STUDENT: You can check it against the pointer on the number line to see if you remembered to punch in the number or not.

DOT: What if your models don't match one another? How are you handling that?

STUDENT: We make them match by using the chart to go back over our game step by step.

Summary Discussion to Deepen Understandings

Dot calls the students together to talk about what they have learned. She makes use of the questions she and Jen planned when they developed the lesson during their summer meetings.

DOT: Why did most people place their first numbers in the tens column?

STUDENT: We filled up with lots of tens, then used our ones at the end.

STUDENT: We tried a few games putting our first numbers in the ones place and couldn't get very close to one hundred at the end.

DOT: How did you decide where to put the small numbers you rolled?

STUDENT: Anything we rolled that was below a three got to be in the tens place.

STUDENT: We chose tens in the beginning if we got four or less.

DOT: How did you use the information from the different models to make your decisions?

STUDENT: We used the hundred grid and the number line to know if we were getting close to one hundred. We didn't want to waste all our spaces.

STUDENT: The chart showed us we already had ten ones and three tens, and we had three turns left.

STUDENT: If we put the number in the tens place, then we had to roll one on the next roll or go bust, and that's hard to do.

Examples of Follow-up Assessment

Dot decides to ask her second graders to use their place-value charts to look back over each of their games to see if they could rearrange their tens and ones to get closer to 100 without going bust. They will use a new recording sheet to show the rearranged numbers and will attach it to their original recording sheet before they turn it in. Dot takes their ideas for rearranging the numbers and adds it to information gleaned from her observations of the group members at work.

Dot's observations identify some children who do not yet trust the idea that grouping objects in different ways to count them yields the same total they get when they count by ones. They still need to recount by ones to verify the quantity. Since she and Jen have identified *One-to-Group Correspondence* as an important prerequisite understanding, she knows that these students will benefit from more opportunities to work with numbers they group in a variety of ways to count—including tens and extras. She decides to give them collections of objects to estimate and then use skip counting to find actual quantities (see Figure E–7 in Appendix E).

Some students show a firm grasp of partitioning by tens and ones. Dot asks them to change the rules of the game as follows and then report how their strategies change as a result:

- How would the game change if you used a ten-sided die or a spinner with the digits zero through nine?
- How would the game change if you could go over 100, or if you could choose to add or subtract? Could you get closer to 100?

Here are some of the students' responses:

- We thought we only got to 71, but look! We only took six turns!! When we rolled again, we got a 4. If we made it four ones, that only gives us 75. But if we made it four tens, that would be 111, which is closer to 100 than 75.
- If I could subtract, I probably would use a lot more tens. But if we had to get an exact number, like 105, I'd be more careful and use more ones.
- I'd go 'til I busted. Then I'd start subtracting, but then I might need more than seven turns.
- If we were in big trouble, we'd subtract. Like if we had 90 and still had lots of turns.

Reflecting on Balancing Instructional Responsibilities

Dot spends some time with Jen after they have both taught the lesson to discuss their observations. Jen starts the conversation. "You know, about half of my class had trouble counting the money to figure out how seven people could have exactly one hundred dollars. I was worried that they weren't ready yet for *100 or Bust!* But when they took turns using all of the models, they seemed to get it! It was fun to watch how they shared the responsibilities."

Dot adds, "I thought the game revealed a lot about which children are ready to think of tens as units and which still have to count by ones. Some of my children were effortlessly switching back and forth between tens and ones. One or two could even do it in their heads. But then they had to explain to their group how they did it, so everyone benefited from their intellectual leap!"

Jen is thoughtful. "You know, I suppose I expected my children to have a real breakthrough. But I guess experiencing one game like *100 or Bust!* is just part of what we will be working on all year long."

Dot smiles at this. "I guess we forget how much intellectual growth is expected of our second graders. Some come to us just teetering on the brink of conserving number, while the expectation is that they will *master* adding and subtracting with regrouping by the end of the year! I guess that's why I am determined to protect them from too much third-grade math content while they are still struggling with the power and patterns of place value. They need time. And we need to plan lots of opportunities for them to develop such an important conceptual understanding."

Dot and Jen get out their planning calendars and continue mapping the rest of the year to make sure they give their second graders the kind of experiences they need and the time to build the understanding of how—with only ten digits—numbers of any size can be represented. What a concept!

Study Questions for Professional Learning Communities

1. Why should a teacher at any grade level think carefully about adding content to address accountability needs for the next grade level?

2. In what ways does an attempt to address the tension between accountability goals and the time needed for understanding impact curricular planning at the classroom level, campus level, and district level?

3. What should you consider when deciding what your students must spend time on to be successful in the next grade?

4. Identify two or three important mathematical ideas to focus on that you really want your students to understand as a result of spending a year with you. Identify or create some items or tasks that will provide you with information about how well they have learned these ideas.

5. Share your items/tasks with colleagues from grade levels immediately below and above you. How do your ideas fit together to provide students with a complex web of interconnected mathematical ideas? How well do these curricular connections address accountability needs?

Connecting Representations to Focus on Deepening Understanding

A Lesson on Multiplication of Whole Numbers

Belinda is a young woman who is preparing for her first year of teaching. Her beginning assignment is grade 3. She is excited about teaching math because in her teacher preparation courses she made some connections that strengthened her own understanding. She wants to recreate that excitement in her students.

Belinda will be working in an urban, inner-city school that is located in what some describe as an unsafe environment. Many of the students do not speak English as a first language, most of them are from low socioeconomic home environments, and many of them have parents who aren't focused on the scholastic abilities of their children, particularly with regard to learning mathematics. For these students, especially, it is critically important to make the purposeful connections that convince them that mathematics makes sense and that they can depend on its patterns and predictability as useful tools in their lives. Being new to the area and the district, Belinda hopes that her university courses and student teaching experience will be enough to see her through her planning for the year. Luckily, she has discovered that her school colleagues are very willing to share their planning and materials from previous years.

Planning for Focused Instruction

Belinda's district has decided that this year they would like to bring more focus to the mathematics curriculum by identifying one idea (or set of related ideas) at each grade level that should receive a high level of attention. In grade 3, it will be multiplication and division. Belinda realizes that this topic is essential for third graders, and she also recognizes that fluency with multiplication and division goes well beyond the ability to remember basic facts. She is familiar with NCTM's (2000) example of a K–grade 8 focused curriculum in mathematics, in which the majority of students bring from grade 2 a well-developed understanding of whole numbers and are expected to leave grade 3 prepared to commit multiplication and division facts to memory in grade 4 (148–156). Therefore, she understands, the grade 3 teacher must not only use the intensive instructional time carved out in that year to help students build understandings of the two operations themselves and practice applying these operations to solve problems, but also provide students with the basis for a new repertoire of basic facts. NCTM (2006) describes a focal point for multiplication and division in grade 3 as follows:

> *Number and Operations* and *Algebra:* Developing understandings of multiplication and division and strategies for basic multiplication facts and related division facts   Students understand the meanings of multiplication and division of whole numbers through the use of representations (e.g., equal-sized groups, arrays, area models, and equal "jumps" on number lines for multiplication, and successive subtraction, partitioning, and sharing for division). They use properties of addition and multiplication (e.g., commutativity, associativity, and the distributive property) to multiply whole numbers and apply increasingly sophisticated strategies based on these properties to solve multiplication and division problems involving basic facts. By comparing a variety of solution strategies, students relate multiplication and division as inverse operations.

In other words, the concepts of multiplication and division are important emerging structures in grade 3, essential for continuing to build complex mathematical understandings.

Belinda and the other grade 3 teachers understand that this focus on multiplication and division does not mean that this is the only mathematics they will teach throughout the year. It means that they must try to spend more time on developing meanings for these ideas and make efforts to use them as often as possible within the contexts of work with other topics such as geometry and measurement and data representation. In her mathematics methods course, Belinda was introduced to the idea of using the diagram of a tree to think about connections in the elementary mathematics curriculum. Now, when she meets with her colleagues to discuss plans for the year, she shares a sample of one from her course (Figure 6–1).

The other teachers recognize most of the ideas that are represented in the tree, and they spend some time talking about how they have dealt with these ideas in previous years. Not all of Belinda's colleagues have used every representation of multiplication mentioned in the tree (e.g., jumps on a number line), and they spend time discussing the strengths and weaknesses of each of the representations, as they perceive them.

Determining the Objective and Rationale for the Lesson

Quite a bit of the third-grade teachers' discussion revolves around the types of representations the teachers have used previously when introducing the idea of multiplication. Everyone agrees that using repeated addition seems to be the easiest way to help students find products for the basic multiplication facts, because the students already understand addition. "So," one teacher asks, "why do we even need to bother with these other ways to show multiplication, like arrays and areas of rectangles? It's just confusing to have different ways of representing the same thing."

Belinda mentally recalls a similar discussion from her methods course, a discussion that she found very interesting because it made her think a little differently about mathematics in general. She shares her thoughts with the group, saying, "When we discussed that question with our mathematics education professor in our methods course, she showed us some things that really made me think about that issue. It really boiled down to two big ideas. First, one way we strengthen our understanding about mathematics is by making connections between ideas that look different on the surface but are really the same mathematically. Second, some representations are more

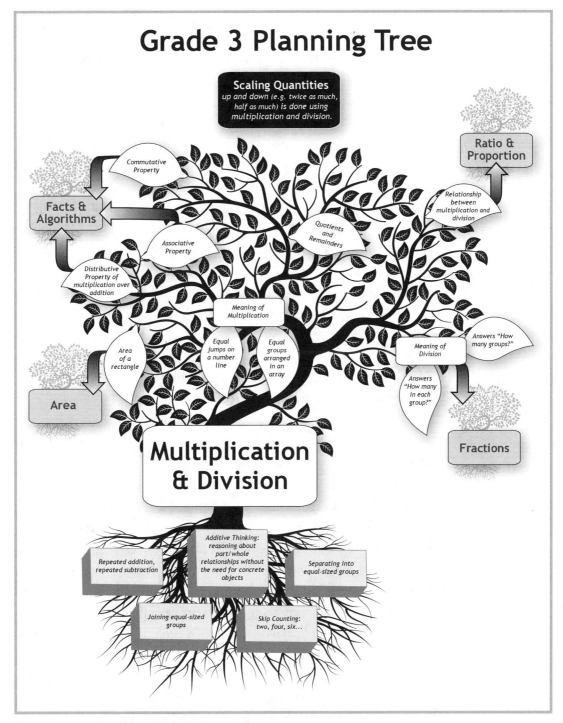

Figure 6–1 Grade 3 Planning Tree for Multiplication and Division

generally useful mathematically than others. For example, finding the total number of items in an array is like repeated addition of a bunch of equal groups because the rows in the array *are* equal groups. But an array only works well for representing whole numbers. If we connect the array model to the area model, then we have a model that can be used for both multiplication of whole numbers now and multiplication with fractions later."

As a result of their discussion, the teachers do a little more research on representations for multiplication (e.g., Fosnot and Dolk 2001a; NCTM 2000; Van de Walle 2007). They see that the different representations appear in the contexts of word problems that students will encounter among the state's assessment items. The teachers decide that it will be valuable for students to recognize all of these as multiplication-type problems, rather than trying to learn to deal with them as separate types of problems. From their research, they decide that they need to start their work on multiplication and division by helping students learn about and build connections between these different representations.

Identifying an Engaging Task, Appropriate Materials, and Questioning Strategies

A major goal of the entire school is to make learning more relevant to students' lives. Therefore, the third-grade teachers always try to introduce new ideas within contexts that are familiar to students from their everyday experiences. The teachers decide to start the activity by asking students to brainstorm about things that come in twos, threes, fours, and so on, so these contexts will be visible right away. They want the rest of the activity to connect the real-world contexts to the more abstract representations for multiplication and build connections among them. Therefore, they design a recording sheet for the activity that requires students to represent a given multiplication situation in a variety of ways: as joining equal groups, as equal jumps on a number line, as a repeated addition equation, as an array, and as a multiplication equation. Students will identify what is common about the representations and practice using the language _____ *groups of* _____. (For the complete lesson plan, see Appendix F.)

The teachers decide that, since this is an introductory activity for development of a major mathematical structure, they need to be able to watch and listen to students as they work with the various representations. The more experienced teachers know some of the misconceptions that can occur with each of the representations, but no one is quite sure how the students will deal with making the connections between representations. They decide to model the activity with the whole class first and then have the students work in pairs to encourage the actions and student talk that the teachers need to see and hear for ongoing assessment and planning for next steps.

As they plan this beginning multiplication activity, the teachers begin to realize that one important characteristic of a focused curriculum is that students must have time to regularly revisit big ideas in order to deepen their understandings. Students cannot learn everything they need to know about the meaning of multiplication in one experience. Therefore, the physical, verbal, and numerical representations of multiplication introduced in this lesson must reappear throughout the year. For example, students can use equal groups (e.g., twos, fives) and skip count to count sets of objects that may occur within the context of collecting data or finding a measurement. And, although this particular lesson emphasizes the meaning of multiplication, the representations and language used need to prepare students for work with division in the near future.

The teachers decide that they will keep the Grade 3 Planning Tree for Multiplication and Division in a prominent place as they design tasks and questions. It will help remind them of the need for laying the groundwork for using multiplication in various contexts and connecting it to related mathematical ideas such as division. They brainstorm some generic questions that will help them stay focused during this lesson and that they can use in other lessons as well. Examples include:

- Can you use equal groups to figure out _____?
- If so, how?
- How many groups do you have?
- How many are in each group?
- How did you figure out how many there are in all?
- Can you draw an array to illustrate this situation?
- If so, what does the array represent?

- What do the rows in the array represent?
- What do the columns in the array represent?
- Can you draw a picture of jumps on a number line to illustrate this situation?
- If so, what do the jumps represent?
- How many jumps do you need to make?
- How big is each jump?

They realize that they will not want to ask every one of these questions in every multiplication situation. However, they do want to try to help students think about different ways to represent their thinking.

Implementing the Focused Instruction

After each of the teachers tries the *Modeling Multiplication* activity in their classroom, they meet to discuss their observations. Since this topic is the year's main focus for grade 3, they have decided to devote some part of each weekly joint planning period to something related to multiplication or division. Of course, the discussion in this planning period ends up being *all* about working with different representations for multiplication.

BELINDA: Whew! In reality, helping students see the connections between different representations wasn't as easy as it sounded in my university course! I think that next time I may put three students in each group so I don't have so many different groups to work with.

LAURA: Well, I ended up having to let most of my students work individually. They all seemed interested when we were brainstorming the things that come in twos, threes, and fours, and everyone was contributing. But then they didn't like sharing the manipulatives. I could look around and see what they were doing, but I don't think I learned very much about what they were thinking, since they only needed to talk when I asked them a specific question.

BISENTE: Mine were talking, but not always about what I wanted to hear, so I needed to ask them some questions anyway. I think we should spend some time today talking about the questions we asked and which ones we thought gave us the most information, so we'll know which ones to keep using in other multiplication activities and which ones to use again next year. We might even be able to think of some more questions to add to our list, now that we have actually done the activity.

BELINDA: It would help me to hear more about the kinds of questions you guys were asking. I'd also like to see some of the things your students did on their recording sheets. Since this is my first year to do anything like this, I really didn't know what to expect.

The teachers decide that they will spend the rest of their planning time discussing questions for embedded assessment and share examples from their follow-up assessment tasks.

Using Embedded Assessment to Support Focused Instruction

As the dialogue shows, the different situations that occurred in the teachers' classrooms gave them some different perspectives on embedded assessment to support focused instruction. The number of small groups that Belinda had to work with kept her from being able to move around enough to get sufficient information from each student. Laura wasn't hearing any student talk, because her students wanted to work independently and weren't experiencing the need to verbalize what they were thinking or to ask questions about what someone else was thinking. Bisente wanted to focus his students' talk more on the mathematics of the activity. The teachers' conversation about the lesson continues.

LAURA: So, Bisente, how did you get your students to talk about their thinking about multiplication?

BISENTE: Well, I started by trying to use those generic questions that we discussed in our previous planning period. It turns out that they helped me remember what the important mathematical ideas were, but I really had to watch what the students were doing in their groups to come up with a question that made sense to them. I ended up asking a lot of *why* questions, such as, "Why did you make the jumps on your number line this size? Why did you put that many blocks in the rows in your array?" And then I had to listen for them to say things that I knew were related to multiplication and point out to them how they were using the basic idea of multiplication, as in "3 groups of 4."

LAURA: Those are questions that you could ask a student working in a group or a student working independently.

BELINDA: I thought it was also very important to ask them how their number line and their array and their number sentences were all alike, since one of our main goals was making connections between the representations. That question sometimes took a long time for a group to answer, because they might not have thought about their work like that yet. That's why I didn't feel like I heard enough from each student. Maybe I need to think next time about a more efficient way to handle those more complex embedded assessment questions, like giving the whole class the question at the same time and letting them discuss it in their groups awhile before I go around to hear their responses. Or maybe they could write about it.

The teachers believe that the sharing of these experiences has helped them think more about the value of embedded assessment questions and how they could be used in a variety of situations.

Summary Discussion to Deepen Understandings

After reviewing their experiences with the lesson, the teachers all agree that the purpose for the summary discussion for this lesson was fairly straightforward—to focus the students' attention on the idea of using multiplication when dealing with equal groups. The summary questions they asked were mainly, "How many groups? How many in each group?" They hope that they reinforced connections by asking the same questions in relation to all of the representations. But, they again remind themselves that they must embed the use of multiplication in various contexts throughout the year to continue to build students' understandings of this important idea and to lay the foundation for future work with division.

BELINDA: I'm going to keep the multiplication and division tree on my desk where I can see it to remind me of our focus, but I am also going to make a little sign with bold multiplication and division symbols on it to make me think, "Can I embed multiplication or division in this activity?" and keep it where I can see it all the time.

LAURA: Good idea! I was just thinking that when we do our mock election this year, we could make groups of three or four or five votes that are alike and use multiplication equations to record the total number of votes for a candidate.

BISENTE: Maybe at our next planning meeting we could talk about some other places in the curriculum that we could make sure to incorporate the use of multiplication- and division-type questions.

Examples of Follow-up Assessment

Since the teachers had designed a recording sheet to highlight the main student understandings that they were focusing on in this activity, they now have common assessment products to discuss. They find that they are able to use the evidences of student thinking that appear on the recording sheets not only to assess individual student understanding but also to reflect on the effectiveness of the lesson itself.

BISENTE: I noticed that when my students started working on their own with the open-ended recording sheet, they had trouble drawing an appropriate array to use. Like when someone picked table legs from the list and rolled a 5, they wanted to draw the same array that was on the worksheet we used in the demonstration to represent five groups of three, instead of drawing an array for five groups of four. I think next time I need to make sure that I emphasize more the connection between the number of squares in each row and the situation it is representing, so that they know what they need to think about to draw their own array. Or maybe I need to model an example with the open-ended worksheet.

BELINDA: Maybe none of my students did that because I was worried that they would get confused, so I just showed each group how to draw the empty array for whatever situation they had chosen. But now I don't know whether they really understand the connection, or if they just followed my directions without understanding them.

LAURA: Bisente, I noticed the same thing that you noticed on several of my students' papers. It seems that they aren't really seeing the connection between the number of items in the rows of the array and the situation in the problem. Perhaps we should remove the array that is printed on the recording sheet for the demonstration so that students have to draw the whole array even during the demo. That way they would have to think about the groups of three that they use to make each row, instead of just deciding how many rows of three to color.

As the teachers leave their planning meeting, they feel like they have made a good start on building into their mathematics instruction a focus on multiplication that will provide a better understanding for their students and that will support connections to future mathematics.

Reflecting on Connecting Multiple Representations

After this discussion of the lesson, Belinda continues to think about the role that representations play in focused mathematics instruction. Although in her preservice courses she learned a lot of different ways to represent many of the ideas that she is expected to teach this year, she now realizes that it takes more than the introduction of these representations to focus her students' thinking on important mathematical ideas. She must consciously and conscientiously plan to help her students understand the important components of each of the representations and make connections among them in order for the important mathematical idea to emerge as the focus of the learning. From her recent experiences, she believes that the benefits of providing her students with opportunities to make these connections outweigh the classroom management issues that are involved, such as distribution of materials, periods of confusion as students explore the materials, and storage space.

Most of Belinda's students will not be able to make these connections from a single lesson on an important idea such as multiplication. Focused instruction on an important concept must occur throughout the year, with students revisiting representations and applications in order to have the multiple experiences they need to build the connections that result in a strong network of understanding.

Study Questions for Professional Learning Communities

Most mathematical ideas can be represented in a variety of ways, such as concrete models, pictures, graphs, words, and numbers.

1. Why is it useful mathematically to understand the connections between two different representations of an idea?
2. Why should you pay attention to helping students make connections among representations when planning instruction?
3. What management issues would you have to deal with to focus instruction on making connections among multiple representations?
4. Identify a topic you teach. What kind of representations would be useful to develop student understanding of this topic?
5. How would you help your students make connections among the different representations to strengthen their understanding?

7

Using Resources Thoughtfully to Focus Instruction

A Lesson on Area Measure

Gloria knows that *area* is one of the topics in her district's grade 4 mathematics curriculum. However, she is concerned that the statement describing the district's learning outcome for grade 4 is too simple—perhaps even boring: "Students will find the area of a rectangle by multiplying length times width." She really wants to make mathematics exciting for her students. In order to find resources to generate their interest, she attends workshops, browses through teaching magazines, and searches on the Internet to find activities that are fun and engaging, with lots of action and movement. She has folders filled with ideas for activities to teach topics such as area—in fact, more activities than students could ever do in any one year, although she tries to include as many as she can. After all, she feels, isn't it important for students to be active and engaged while they are learning math?

This year, due to some special funding provided by the state, Gloria is fortunate to have a math coach available to her. She will have scheduled meetings with Gwen, her math coach, periodically throughout the year; she can also set up additional meetings as needed or communicate electronically for just-in-time support. As Gloria plans for the lessons on area, she contacts Gwen, hoping to add even more interesting activities to her collection. She is slightly disappointed that instead of talking about activities,

Gwen wants to talk about the content itself. However, Gloria quickly engages in the conversation.

Gloria and Gwen discuss the idea that area is usually the first type of measurement that students encounter that can be made *indirectly*, or computed, from other types of measurements. Gloria knows that, as a measurable attribute, area can be determined in the same way as all measurements—by first identifying the particular attribute to be measured (i.e., the amount of surface covered by the shape), then identifying a standard unit with that attribute (e.g., a square inch or square centimeter); and finally comparing the unit to the object to be measured to determine how many of the units it takes to *match* the object (i.e., how many square units are needed to cover the surface of the shape). Gloria summarizes this idea by saying that "the area of a shape can be determined by actually laying out unit squares and counting how many square units it takes to cover the shape completely." Gwen agrees with Gloria's summary and points out that there are mathematical processes that can do this counting for us. For example, in a rectangle, if the squares are aligned in straight rows and columns, like an array showing equal groups, we can use multiplication to find the total number of squares rather than counting them one by one (see Figure 7–1). Their conversation continues as follows:

GWEN: Have you noticed, Gloria, that the length of one dimension of the rectangle tells how many squares are in each row of the array, and the length of the other dimension of the rectangle tells how many squares are in each column? So, in a rectangle like this one I've drawn here, we can find the area by measuring the *length* of each dimension and multiplying these two lengths together.

GLORIA: I've noticed that my students often will ask me if they need to add or multiply when we are working with rectangles. I guess they are confusing finding perimeter and finding area.

GWEN: Well, they are definitely confusing the processes for determining the measurements of these two very different attributes. Perimeter is a length and is measured with pieces of length, like inches or centimeters. Area is measured with pieces of area, like square inches or square centimeters. If a student does not have a good understanding

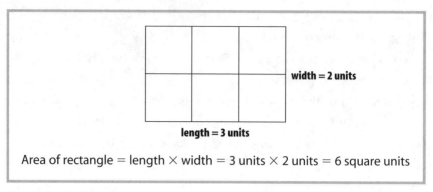

width = 2 units

length = 3 units

Area of rectangle = length × width = 3 units × 2 units = 6 square units

Figure 7–1   3-by-2 Array

of the attribute of area and the type of unit that is used to measure area, then being told to *measure the sides and multiply them together* to find area may make it seem like the attribute they are finding is length. It just shows that the meaningful development of the formula for finding the area of rectangles is a critical mathematical concept. It lays the groundwork for later work with more complex area and volume formulas. Perhaps you can select from your resources activities that focus on the development of the area formula for a rectangle.

Planning for Focused Instruction

After talking with Gwen, Gloria returns to her planning with some new thoughts about teaching area. As she looks through her resources, she finds that NCTM (2006) describes a focal point for learning about area measurement in Grade 4 as follows:

Measurement: Developing an understanding of area and determining the areas of two-dimensional shapes   Students recognize area as an attribute of two-dimensional regions. They learn that they can quantify area by finding the total number of same-sized units of area that cover the shape without gaps or overlaps. They understand that a square 1 unit on a side is the standard unit for measuring area. They select appropriate units, strategies (e.g., decomposing shapes), and tools for solving problems that involve estimating or measuring area. Students connect area measure to the area model that they have used to represent multiplication, and they use this connection to justify the formula for the area of a rectangle. (16)

Gloria believes that if she builds her instruction around this description, her students can develop a strong understanding of area measure. In addition, she plans to help them deepen their understanding of linear measure from earlier experiences by identifying how the two types of measurement are alike and different.

To make the unit on area active and engaging, Gloria pulls out all the stops. She sets up activity stations around the room, where students will find areas of different shapes of rectangles in many different contexts. Students get plenty of practice multiplying length times width. Then, a couple of days into the unit of study, one of Gloria's students asks *the* question: "Miss Gottlieb, last year we did a thing called *perimeter*, where we added the lengths and widths of rectangles. Now we're multiplying them. How do you know when to add them or when to multiply them?"

In the past, Gloria's response to this question would have been, "Well, you add them when you are finding perimeter, and you multiply them when you are finding area." However, since her discussion with Gwen, she realizes that this student's need for understanding goes deeper. It is a question about the basic difference between the two attributes of perimeter and area, as well as a question about the different methods for computing each type of measurement. Gloria now realizes that if the students understood the attributes themselves, then the different computational methods (adding or multiplying) would automatically make sense. And she is pretty sure that if one student has this question, others do also.

So, how can she address the question now from this deeper perspective? To determine whether or not it is an important issue affecting other students, she spends some time the next day asking individual students some questions as they work at the activity stations. For example, she talks with one student who is working through the activities quickly and accurately:

GLORIA: Carrie, I see you've done several of the activities already. What were you measuring each time?

CARRIE: I was measuring lengths and widths.

GLORIA: How did you find those measurements?

CARRIE: With a ruler.

GLORIA: Why did you measure the lengths and widths?

CARRIE: So I could multiply them together.

GLORIA: And why did you multiply them together?

CARRIE: Because that gives you the area.

GLORIA: The area of what?

CARRIE: The shapes, the rectangles.

GLORIA: So, how would you describe the area of a shape?

CARRIE: The length times the width.

With a burst of insight, Gloria then asks Carrie, "So does a triangle or a circle have area?"

Carrie replies, "I guess it could, if you knew how to measure its length and width." Gloria wonders now if Carrie really understands the result of multiplying a rectangle's length times its width.

After Gloria has several of these types of conversations with students as they work, she realizes that although all of the students are active and engaged in finding areas of rectangles, few of them can articulate what they are actually representing when they find the product of length times width. Although she knows that her students have done activities in earlier grades that involved covering shapes with triangles or squares and talking about area, they are not connecting the process of computing area in these activities to the meaning of area as a measurable attribute. She is disappointed that her collection of activities isn't doing the job. Gloria emails Gwen, and they decide that she needs to bring the class together for some whole-group discussion that focuses on this connection.

Determining the Objective and Rationale for the Lesson

To prepare for a whole-class lesson on area, Gloria does a little reading in her textbook support materials. She also looks back at some of her workshop notes from the discussions the participants had after doing some of the activities. With Gwen's help, she makes a list of important ideas about the general process of measurement, area measure in particular, and the process of computing the area of a rectangle. They work together to create the Grade 4 Planning Tree for Area in Figure 7–2.

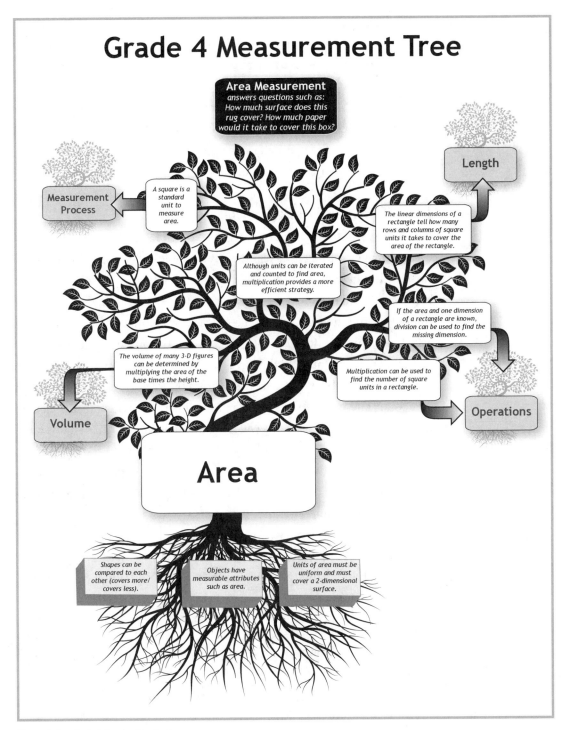

Grade 4 Measurement Tree

Area Measurement answers questions such as: How much surface does this rug cover? How much paper would it take to cover this box?

Length

A square is a standard unit to measure area.

Measurement Process

The linear dimensions of a rectangle tell how many rows and columns of square units it takes to cover the area of the rectangle.

Although units can be iterated and counted to find area, multiplication provides a more efficient strategy.

If the area and one dimension of a rectangle are known, division can be used to find the missing dimension.

The volume of many 3-D figures can be determined by multiplying the area of the base times the height.

Multiplication can be used to find the number of square units in a rectangle.

Volume

Operations

Area

Shapes can be compared to each other (covers more/ covers less).

Objects have measurable attributes such as area.

Units of area must be uniform and must cover a 2-dimensional surface.

Figure 7–2 Grade 4 Planning Tree for Area

Gloria and Gwen decide that Gloria should focus on the general meaning of area and the specific use of the linear dimensions of a rectangle to compute its area. She wants her students to be able to answer this question: "How can making two linear measurements tell you how many square units of area are needed to cover a rectangle?" Gloria also wants her students to be comfortable with the difference between using length and width to calculate the perimeter of a rectangle and using length and width to calculate the area of a rectangle.

Identifying an Engaging Task, Appropriate Materials, and Questioning Strategies

Gloria's biggest struggle in planning this whole-class lesson is giving up some of her favorite activities. When she and Gwen had looked through her area activities from this new perspective—developing meaning for computing the area of a rectangle—she began to see that many of the activities were good for practicing the process of computing area, but they did not contribute much to the development of its meaning. Now she also realizes that for this type of focused attention to occur in a whole-group discussion, she needs to use a more formal instructional guide. So she and Gwen decide that the students will work in small groups, on the same fairly simple activity that builds an obvious connection between the dimensions of a rectangle and the number of squares it takes to cover it. Gwen helps her outline the types of questions she wants to ask students as they work in their small groups and after they have finished the activity.

In the activity, students will be using square tiles to build rectangles (see the full lesson plan in Appendix G). Gloria plans to ask her students the following questions as they are working to focus their attention on the objectives of the activity:

- What is the perimeter of the rectangle? How do you know?
- What part of the grid or tiles do you count to determine the perimeter?
- What is the area of the rectangle? How do you know?
- What part of the grid or tiles do you count to determine the area?
- What part of the grid or tiles tells you the length and width of the rectangle? How do those relate to the perimeter?

- What relationship do you notice in your table between the length and width of the rectangle and the number of squares in, or area of, the rectangle?

At the end of the lesson, to focus students' attention on what they should have learned about the relationship of rectangular area to multiplication, she plans to ask questions such as:

- What does the length of a rectangle describe about the squares covering it?
- What does the width of a rectangle describe about the squares covering it?
- What do the squares covering the rectangle measure?
- How do the squares covering the rectangle compare to an array?
- How do we use multiplication to count the number of objects in an array?
- Is it true in our examples that length times width of the rectangle is equal to the number of squares covering the rectangle? How is this related to the area of the rectangle?
- Does it make sense mathematically that we multiply the length times the width of a rectangle to find its area?
- How do we write the area of the rectangle so that we know that it is a measurement describing area?

With these suggested questions in mind, Gloria and Gwen feel that she will be better prepared to focus her students' attention and help them profit as much as possible from the whole-class experience.

Implementing the Focused Instruction

Gloria introduces the lesson and walks around the classroom as her students work in small groups to build rectangles. She carries a note card with her to remind her of the types of questions she wants to ask them as they work. As she prompts them to think about how the dimensions of the rectangle relate to the arrays formed by the tiles, she realizes that she is actually preparing her students to respond to the summary questions that she has planned for the end of the lesson. At first, she feels like she is giving away the answers to the test, but then she realizes that perhaps her feeling is the result of focusing instruction on a pre-identified learning outcome. She makes a quick note to herself to talk to Gwen about this feeling.

Using Embedded Assessment to Support Focused Instruction

Gloria is a little surprised at first that her students become so engaged, even though she has only provided them with one fairly simple activity. As the lesson progresses and she continues to probe students' abilities to connect the multiplication to the process of determining the number of squares needed to cover the rectangle, she begins to see the need for some differentiated levels of engagement. She sends students who indicate they have made this connection to some of the stations she has set up to continue to explore area in a variety of settings. She continues to work with students who are having difficulties answering her questions about this connection. In this way, her students are still getting some differentiated instruction within the whole-class activity. Gloria remembers that Gwen mentioned using the questions they created as embedded assessment, so she makes a note to ask more about ways to do this.

Summary Discussion to Deepen Understandings

Gloria is reluctant to pull students away from what they are working on, but she believes it is critical to bring the class back together as a whole group to discuss the summary questions that focus on the critical objectives that she and Gwen identified. Although she and Gwen prepared a list of questions together, Gloria decides to use them with her students a little differently to assess their understanding. To begin, she draws a ten-inch by twelve-inch rectangle on the board, labels its dimensions, and asks if there is anyone in the class who would like to describe the area of the rectangle.

STUDENT: It is one hundred and twenty.

GLORIA: Yes, remember we say one hundred twenty. Does anyone want to add to that description?

STUDENT: One hundred twenty squares.

GLORIA: What kind of squares?

STUDENT: These kind. [Student holds up an inch tile.]

GLORIA: So, I understand from you showing me that tile that you are saying that one hundred twenty of those tiles will fit into this rectangle. How would you tell me if you didn't have it to show to me?

STUDENT: One hundred twenty square inches, because the tile is an inch on each side.

GLORIA: Now I would be able to understand without you showing me the tile. How did you know that one hundred twenty of them would be needed to cover this rectangle without actually putting them all in there?

STUDENT: You can fit twelve of them across the bottom of the rectangle. And then you can make ten rows of twelve to fill up the rectangle.

GLORIA: How did you know that twelve of them would fit across?

STUDENT: Because that side is twelve inches long.

GLORIA: And how did you know that you could make ten rows?

STUDENT: Because the other side is ten inches long.

GLORIA: And how did you figure out that you would use one hundred twenty tiles?

STUDENTS: We multiplied!

Gloria isn't sure that everyone has truly made the connection. She wants to continue with questions about how the area would change if the rectangle's dimensions were in centimeters instead of inches, or what would happen if they had a rectangle whose dimensions weren't whole numbers of units. But she decides to save those questions for students to explore in their center activities, as they continue to deepen their understanding of area measure.

Examples of Follow-up Assessment

Gloria has talked with Gwen about the importance of preparing her students for formal assessments as mandated by the state. Although she still wants to provide opportunities for her students to explore the concept of area with open-ended questions, she recognizes that they also need to have practice answering more specific questions about area. She decides to give them the following assessment-type items to respond to and discuss:

1. Given rectangles with the following dimensions, determine the area of each rectangle.
   a. 13 cm by 5 cm   b. 10 cm by 10 cm   c. 24 cm by 3 cm
2. If a rectangle has an area of 36 square inches, what could its length and width be?
3. If a rectangle has an area of 56 square inches and its length is 8 inches, what is its width?

Gloria might even have her students use grid paper to model their solutions to the problems, as a form of self-checking and as a way to connect these items to the models that they have been using during class.

Reflecting on the Thoughtful Use of Resources

Although Gloria began with the idea that the more activities she could cram into an instructional session the better, her observations of her students and her work with her math coach led her to change her thinking. Although her students were engaged in the many activities she had provided for them, she found that it was possible that they were not paying attention to the important ideas that were necessary for moving on in the mathematics. By narrowing her selection of resources, providing students with a common experience, and using specifically designed questions during and after the experience, Gloria was able to focus her instruction and her students' learning to better prepare them for future investigations of this topic. The time she spent on the activity in this lesson this year was much longer than she had ever spent, but she also feels that she has much more information about the levels of understanding in her students. Since she knows that her students need to revisit the idea of area throughout the year to strengthen their understanding, she plans to sift through her many activities and identify the ones that will be the most beneficial to them in terms of everyone's time and effort.

Study Questions for Professional Learning Communities

1. What is the purpose of having a variety of resources available for designing instruction?

2. How do you decide which activities you want to add to your collection of resources?

3. How do you decide which activities to use in a particular lesson?

4. Think of a math concept for which you have lots of activities available. Which of the activities are worth your time (and your students' time)? Which of these activities are fun but not very rich mathematically? Which ones address conceptual development? And which ones provide challenging applications? Justify your choices.

5. If you could use only one of these activities to focus your students' thinking on this important mathematical idea, which one would you choose? Why?

Beyond Worksheets

*A Lesson on Connecting Geometry
and Measurement*

Corrie has been teaching fifth grade for a number of years, including eight years in her current district—a small, rural community. School events are poorly attended; teachers often outnumber the parents. Corrie and her colleagues are often frustrated by their attempts to enlist parental support. Students are not reliable about practicing skills or completing assignments outside of school hours. Occasionally—fortunately not frequently—parents express hostility about how the school is trying to alienate their children and change their way of life.

For a number of years, Corrie had been teaching from a very traditional textbook that provided a script for the teacher, lots of worksheets, and very specific, lockstep expectations for students. Although most of her students were able to complete the worksheet exercises, Corrie was haunted by their lack of interest or motivation. She was also uncertain that their correct answers on worksheets provided reliable evidence of deep, mathematical understanding.

Two summers ago, Corrie attended a regional math conference for the first time. She discovered sessions that introduced her to ways of teaching that were very different from how she remembered being taught mathematics when she was in school. She came to realize that she was teaching mathematics in very much the same way she had been taught. She also became acquainted with a couple of teachers from other school districts—

Belinda and Gloria. Together, they attended a session on the NCTM Curriculum Focal Points. At the end of the conference, they vowed to stay in touch electronically and share ideas, worries, and excitement.

As a result of those experiences, Corrie decided to try a few lessons built around some thought-provoking mathematical investigations. Adapting some activities she received from Belinda and Gloria, Corrie introduced her students to some meaningful, real-world situations. She was amazed to see brief flickers of interest behind the eyes of many of her students. This—along with encouragement from her new friends—gave her the courage to approach her principal with a proposal to revamp her mathematics program around the Curriculum Focal Points. After several meetings and quite a few side-by-side comparisons between her state standards and the Focal Points, Corrie received the go-ahead to implement some carefully planned units of study. "After all," remarked her principal, "our math scores have no way to go but *up*!"

Planning for Focused Instruction

This past spring break, Corrie studied district test results and confirmed what she suspected. Through the years, the weakest areas for fifth graders have been measurement (specifically perimeter, area, and volume) and division. Further reading supported her findings. She read about a study in which students received pictures of rectangular prisms and were asked to estimate the volume. The students often counted just the squares they could see in the illustrations, ignoring the cubes hidden in the middle of the prism and double or triple counting the cubes in the corners (Battista 2003). She also discovered in a 1986 article by Janet Shroyer and William Fitzgerald that this is not a new problem: "Students' incorrect responses and the nature of their errors to relatively simple questions involving area, perimeter, surface area, and volume continue to dismay those who examine [NAEP] test results" (2). Because students tend to think of measurement as applying formulas rather than considering the number of squares that will cover a surface or the number of cubes that will fill a container, they need many different hands-on experiences finding area and volume to alleviate this confusion.

In addition to the discoveries Corrie has made from the research she has read and the data she has analyzed, she knows other disturbing things about her students. They don't feel very smart and have become convinced that only smart people can be good in math. They don't see math as useful. Instead, they see it as a collection of disconnected facts and procedures that are not expected to make sense—just to be memorized. Although it would be easy to be discouraged, Corrie is not about to give up on her fifth graders. She sees the NCTM Curriculum Focal Points as a way of organizing her instruction around mathematical big ideas that are connected and full of patterns. She feels it is up to her to plan meaningful, rich mathematical experiences for her students. She wants to help them notice emerging patterns and to think about how these patterns can uncover important foundational mathematical understandings.

The NCTM Curriculum Focal Points (2006) include the following at Grade 5:

Geometry and *Measurement* and *Algebra:* Describing three-dimensional shapes and analyzing their properties, including volume and surface area—Students relate two-dimensional shapes to three-dimensional shapes and analyze properties of polyhedral solids, describing them by the number of edges, faces, or vertices as well as the types of faces. Students recognize volume as an attribute of three-dimensional space. They understand that they can quantify volume by finding the total number of same-sized units of volume that they need to fill the space without gaps or overlaps. They understand that a cube that is 1 unit on an edge is the standard unit for measuring volume. They select appropriate units, strategies, and tools for solving problems that involve estimating or measuring volume. They decompose three-dimensional shapes and find surface areas and volumes of prisms. As they work with surface area, they find and justify relationships among the formulas for the areas of different polygons. They measure necessary attributes of shapes to use area formulas to solve problems.

Corrie's state mathematics standards include:

Geometry and spatial reasoning. The student generates geometric definitions using critical attributes. The student is expected to identify essential attributes including parallel, perpendicular, and congruent parts of two- and three-dimensional geometric figures.

Measurement. The student applies measurement concepts involving length (including perimeter), area, capacity/volume, and weight/mass to solve problems. The student is expected to:

- connect models for perimeter, area, and volume with their respective formulas; and
- select and use appropriate units and formulas to measure length, perimeter, area, and volume.

Although surface area is not taught until grade 8 in her state, Corrie has decided to include it in her unit as an extension investigation—primarily because of its potential for applying the operations of addition, multiplication, and division.

Determining the Objective and Rationale for the Lesson

Corrie spent the summer planning a unit of study in which students use multiplication and division to investigate the volume and surface area of rectangular prisms. She was in constant contact with Belinda and Gloria, who were also in the process of developing units and lessons guided not only by the Focal Points, but also by planning trees they had discovered in a session at the state math conference. Belinda sent Corrie a Grade 3 Planning Tree for Multiplication and Division (Figure 6–1). Gloria sent her a Grade 4 Planning Tree for Area (Figure 7–1). Corrie decided to adapt Gloria's Planning Tree for Area for her Grade 5 Planning Tree for Volume (Figure 8–1).

Near the end of the summer, Corrie begins to plan her unit of study. She has identified the following objectives for her lessons in the unit.

The student understands the following:

- Measurement is the process of:
  - Identifying the attribute being measured (such as *volume*);
  - Selecting an appropriate unit (such as a cube);
  - Making an estimate (such as, "About how many cubes do you think it will take to fill the box?");
  - Comparing the unit to the object being measured (such as filling the box with layers of cubes); and

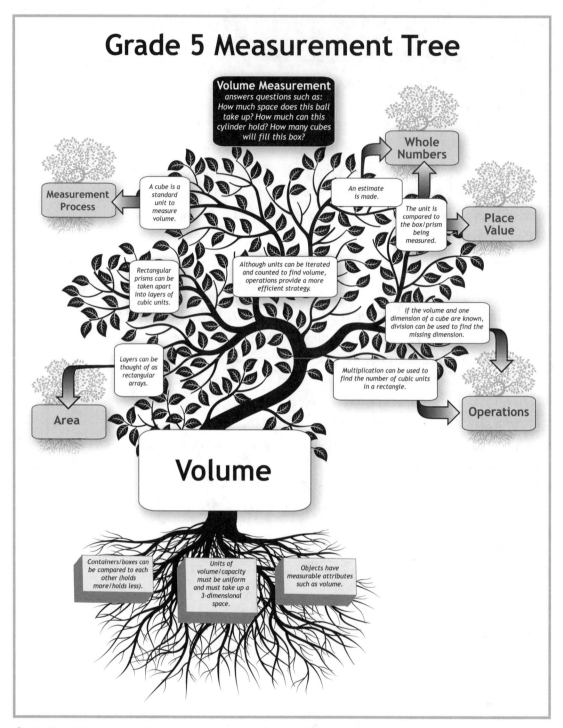

Grade 5 Measurement Tree

Volume Measurement
*answers questions such as:
How much space does this ball
take up? How much can this
cylinder hold? How many cubes
will fill this box?*

Whole Numbers

Measurement Process

A cube is a standard unit to measure volume.

An estimate is made.

The unit is compared to the box/prism being measured.

Place Value

Rectangular prisms can be taken apart into layers of cubic units.

Although units can be iterated and counted to find volume, operations provide a more efficient strategy.

If the volume and one dimension of a cube are known, division can be used to find the missing dimension.

Layers can be thought of as rectangular arrays.

Multiplication can be used to find the number of cubic units in a rectangle.

Area

Operations

Volume

Containers/boxes can be compared to each other (holds more/holds less).

Units of volume/capacity must be uniform and must take up a 3-dimensional space.

Objects have measurable attributes such as volume.

Figure 8–1　Grade 5 Planning Tree for Volume

- Reporting the number of units (such as, "The box holds sixty-four cubic units").
- Volume is a measurable attribute of three-dimensional space.
- A cube is the standard unit of volume because it takes up three-dimensional space, and cubic units must also be uniform in size.
- Surface area is the two-dimensional outside covering of a three-dimensional object.
- A square is the standard unit for measuring surface area because it is also two-dimensional, and squares used for this purpose must be uniform in size.
- A prism is a three-dimensional geometric figure with two congruent parallel polygonal bases. A right rectangular prism has three pairs of parallel faces that are all rectangles. Just as a square is a special rectangle, a cube is a special rectangular prism in which all faces are congruent squares.
- Skill must be used to compare units of volume/area to an object being measured—no gaps, no overlaps.
- Estimation can be used to predict *about* how many units of volume it will take to fill a box or to build a rectangular prism with interlocking cubes.
- Although units can be iterated and counted to find volume, the operations of multiplication and division provide more efficient strategies.

Identifying an Engaging Task, Appropriate Materials, and Questioning Strategies

Over time, Corrie has come to realize that the math script in the textbook she has been following for years is deadly dull. She is determined to plan interesting tasks and to have thought-provoking clusters of questions ready to spark the interest and probe the thinking of her students. To accomplish this goal, she plans a lesson comprising part of her unit on using multiplication and division to investigate geometry, volume, and surface area (see the full lesson plan in Appendix H).

In this lesson, students will use cubic units to estimate and find the volume of a variety of rectangular prisms. They will organize their work to look for patterns and make generalizations. Students will analyze how multiplication and division can be used in investigations involving volume. In a follow-up lesson, students will investigate how volume and surface area change as dimensions change.

Implementing the Focused Instruction

After what seemed like months of planning, Corrie is ready to begin teaching her unit. Since motivation and mathematical relevance is a problem for her students, she puts up a blank bulletin board with two questions: Why find volume? What questions might we be trying to answer? In this way, she is asking students to find real-world reasons to measure volume. They must frame the reasons as questions they can put on the bulletin board.

When Corrie gives the assignment to her first class, asking them to answer the two questions, she is not surprised to encounter stunned silence. She waits. "You may want to talk about the assignment with your group and ask any questions you might have," she advises them. The conversations begin. As Corrie circulates among the groups, she notices that there are still blank looks and frowns of frustration on her students' faces.

CORRIE: What questions do you have?

STUDENT: We're not sure what volume is.

STUDENT: I think it's sort of like area, but bigger.

STUDENT: We think it's like putting stuff into something—like a jar or a box.

CORRIE: Good! We are beginning to define terms—a great place to start! Let's remember some other attributes we have measured in the past, such as how tall we are or how long the hallway is. What tools did we use to do this?

STUDENT: We used measuring tapes and meter sticks.

CORRIE: Measuring tapes and meter sticks are tools used to measure length or distance—even if it isn't straight, such as the border for the bulletin board or the edge around the table. What about when we had to find out how much paper we needed to cover the bulletin board? Or whether our new rug would fit into the space between the bookcase and the chalkboard? What tools did we use then?

STUDENT: I remember we counted the floor tiles to see if the rug would fit. We knew that they are one-foot squares, so we could tell how much of the floor the rug should cover before it bumped into the wall under the chalkboard. Then we cut out one-foot squares and laid them on the rug to see if it was too big for the space.

STUDENT: We used the meter stick again for the bulletin board. But we measured two things—how wide it is and how tall.

CORRIE: Then what did we do?

STUDENT: I remember! We multiplied!

CORRIE: Right! We knew from our geometry unit that the bulletin board is a polygon. One of the attributes of polygons is that they are all two-dimensional. You just mentioned the two dimensions we measured—its width and height. When we multiplied the two dimensions, we found units of area. Measuring area requires us to use a two-dimensional unit such as the square floor tile. Remember that we labeled our measurement *square feet* or *square meters.*

If length is a one-dimensional attribute and area can be thought of as covering a two-dimensional surface, how might we characterize the attributes of things like the jar or box you mentioned earlier?

STUDENT: I know! A jar and a box are three-dimensional!

CORRIE: Yes! So what kind of units will we need to measure something that is three-dimensional?

STUDENT: We'll need three-dimensional units!

CORRIE: Exactly. We have two different kinds of three-dimensional units. When we want to find out how much a jar holds, we usually use units such as fluid ounces, cups, pints, quarts, gallons, and liters. When we measure with these units, we often call the attribute *capacity*. Sometimes when we want to find how much space something takes up, we use cubes—cubic meters, cubic inches, and so forth. Then we often call the attribute *volume.* On our bulletin board, we will focus on using cubic units to measure volume.

Corrie concludes the day's lesson by summarizing their classroom discussion:

- Volume involves measuring how much space something takes up.
- To do this, we use three-dimensional units such as cubes.

Each of Corrie's classes leave that day expressing some interest in measuring volume—three-dimensional space. She had not expected miracles, but is encouraged by the interest they've shown. Unfortunately, she had no idea the "brief review of measurement" she described in her lesson plan would take an entire class period! However, Corrie feels it is worth the extra day because the students obviously needed to focus on the differences between attributes and units of length, area, and volume.

The next day, Corrie reminds her students that they are going to use three-dimensional units to find volume. She distributes interlocking cubes to each group and gives the assignment to her students (also see Figure H–1 in Appendix H):

- Students will use interlocking cubes to build a variety of rectangular prisms (including cubes).
- For each one, they will record:
  - The dimensions of the prism (e.g., $2 \times 3 \times 4$)
  - The volume of the prism (i.e., the number of cubes it took to build it)
- Students will organize the data into a chart.
- tudents will look for patterns in the chart data and use the patterns to make conjectures about finding the volume of any rectangular prism.

Corrie asks her students to draw pictures of their prisms on isometric dot paper (see Figure H–2 in Appendix H) so they can use the drawings for further investigations.

Using Embedded Assessment to Support Focused Instruction

As students work, Corrie asks the questions she prepared ahead of time:

CORRIE: How are you figuring out the volume of each of your prisms? Are you counting the cubes or did you come up with a shortcut?

STUDENT: We just started building prisms and counted the cubes as we built them.

STUDENT: We decided to start with small prisms and then add to them. We added to find the new volume each time.

STUDENT: Angie showed us a shortcut. We can build prisms with layers. She said we could just count the cubes in one layer and then multiply by the number of layers to find the volume. So we tried it, and it worked!

CORRIE: I see your group is building a really big prism. What will you do if you run out of cubes?

STUDENT: We already ran out of cubes! And no one will give us any! So we just decided to draw pictures of each layer.

Summary Discussion to Deepen Understandings

Corrie continues with a summary discussion:

CORRIE: How many different prisms did you build? How did you know each was different?

STUDENT: We all started building prisms. Then we turned them around to see if any were alike. If so, we just added layers of cubes or took some away to make them different.

STUDENT: We were able to build a *ton* of prisms! But we had to take them apart to build new ones. We wrote down the dimensions and volumes.

STUDENT: Shereka made us get organized so we wouldn't waste time. She told us to write down the dimensions first and if the dimensions were different, we decided the prisms would be.

CORRIE: Did that work?

STUDENT: Well, we figured out that the order of the numbers didn't matter. A 3 by 5 by 2 prism is the same as a 2 by 3 by 5 prism. But if the numbers were different, the prisms were different.

STUDENT: Our group started with cubes. We decided to build and draw, build and draw so we wouldn't run out of cubes. Besides, the dot paper was really fun, so we didn't have to keep building them. We could just draw them. [See Figure 8–2.]

STUDENT: But, it was hard to *just* draw them to find the volume. We kept forgetting about the cubes in the middle that we couldn't see from the outside.

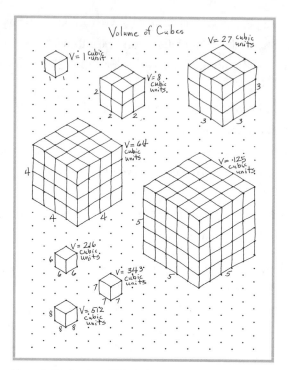

Figure 8–2 Drawings of Cubes on Isometric Dot Paper

STUDENT: Some of our prisms had the same volume. So we decided to pick a volume and see how many prisms we could make with the same volume. And you know what? We thought that the bigger the volume, the more prisms there would be. But that's not what happened. We are still working on it, okay?

Corrie smiles at this. She would never have predicted that her students would want to keep working on a math project! She replies, "Of course it's okay. Be sure to keep a record of all the prisms you build, though, so you can save your hard work. Remember that other classes are still working on this, and they will need to reuse the cubes to keep building prisms."

At this point, Corrie realizes how many different directions this lesson's summary discussion can take. Although many productive discussion points flit through her mind, she decides to keep the focus on how multiplication and division are used to investigate volume. She asks a couple of questions to get the discussion back on track.

CORRIE: Did you have enough interlocking cubes to build each of your prisms? If you ran out, how did you handle this?

STUDENT: We used multiplication to figure out what the bottom layer was.

CORRIE: How did multiplication help you do this?

STUDENT: We remembered about arrays and multiplied the number of rows by the number in each row. Then all we had to do is build *one* row straight up to figure out how tall we wanted our prism to be. We multiplied the cubes in one layer by the number of layers to get the volume of our big prism.

STUDENT: We didn't need to build each prism after we figured out the patterns.

CORRIE: What do you mean?

STUDENT: Well, if you know the number of cubes in the bottom layer, you can just keep adding the number of cubes in each layer to find the volume.

CORRIE: You mentioned adding the layers to find the volume. Did anyone use a different operation?

STUDENT: We multiplied.

CORRIE: How did you decide which numbers to multiply?

STUDENT: We thought of each layer as an array and multiplied the two dimensions to get the number of cubes in the layer. Then we multiplied that number by the number of layers and *ta-dum*, we had the volume.

CORRIE: How did you organize your data on your chart?

STUDENT: We forgot to make a chart. So we had to go back and remember our prisms.

STUDENT: Our chart has two labels—dimensions and volume. We decided to put it on notebook paper first so we could put it in order before we made our big chart. [See Figure 8–3.]

CORRIE: How did you put your data in order?

STUDENT: We started with our little prisms and then kept going.

STUDENT: We started listing all the prisms that had one as one of the dimensions. Then we listed all the prisms that had two as one of the dimensions, and so forth.

Data for Prisms

Dimensions	Volume
1 × 2 × 3	6
2 × 3 × 4	24
2 × 4 × 5	40
3 × 5 × 4	60

Figure 8–3   Data for Prisms

CORRIE: What did you notice as you did this?

STUDENT: Well, the volume kept getting bigger. But that's about all.

CORRIE: Did anyone organize their data a different way? Did a different way to organize the data cause different patterns to emerge?

STUDENT: We decided to group our prisms by their volumes. That's when we discovered several different prisms with the same volume. [See Figure 8–4.]

CORRIE: I wonder how many different prisms you could build with that same volume? How will you know when you have found all of the prisms with that volume?

STUDENT: That's one of the questions we are still trying to answer. We need more time.

CORRIE: If you know the number of cubes it takes to build a prism—that is, its volume—can you figure out its dimensions?

STUDENT: We tried that. We noticed that we could use some of our divisibility rules to try out different numbers. But then, when we found one possible dimension, we still had to do something with the number that was left. It was too big to be one of the dimensions. We sort of got bogged down and gave up.

Corrie is ecstatic! They remember the Divisibility Rules and are making the connection to volume! Imagine!

Corrie continues, "Does anyone have an idea how this group could get *unstuck*? Silence reigns while the students think about the problem. "Why not talk it over with your group and see what you can come up with." Corrie then notices the time. "Oops! We have to wrap this up for today.

Prisms = 24 cubic units

Figure 8–4   Drawings of Prisms on Isometric Dot Paper

Let's hold this question over until tomorrow. We will start first thing with this problem: *If you know the volume of a prism, how can you figure out its dimensions?"*

The next day, Corrie revisits the question from the day before. She has decided to help them get started by asking students to separate their data into two parts—data for cubes and data for other rectangular prisms. After students have reorganized their sets of data, she asks them to compare and contrast them.

> CORRIE: How do the dimensions change in each of your cubes? How about the volumes?
>
> STUDENT: We used a chart to organize our data. [See Figure 8–5.] We listed the dimensions on the left and the volume on the right. We noticed that the volume got really big really fast!

Data for Cubes

Dimensions	Volume
$1 \times 1 \times 1$	1
$2 \times 2 \times 2$	8
$3 \times 3 \times 3$	27
$4 \times 4 \times 4$	64

Figure 8–5   Data for Cubes

STUDENT: We got tired of building cubes after the third one and decided just to multiply the dimensions to get the volume.

CORRIE: How did you know that multiplying the dimensions would give you the volume?

STUDENT: Because yesterday we talked about the *shortcut* of using arrays of rows and columns to find the number of cubes in one layer and then multiplying that number of cubes by the number of layers to get the volume. Jolene noticed that the numbers we used are the same numbers in the dimensions. Then we figured out why we were using $\times$'s when we wrote down the dimensions. That means we have to multiply the numbers together! *Duh!* So we did it and it worked every time.

CORRIE: So could we turn your discovery into a formula for finding the volume of rectangular prisms?

STUDENT: Sure! All we have to do is decide what to call each of the numbers in the dimensions. We came up with *length* times *width* for finding area. How about *length* times *width* times *height*?

CORRIE: Done! Let's add that formula to our formula poster [writes $l \times w \times h$].

CORRIE: What did you discover about finding the dimensions of a cube when you know the volume? Were you able to do it? Explain how.

STUDENT: It was pretty easy. We just took the volume of one of our cubes (like 125 cubic units) and pretended that we didn't already know its dimensions. We used our divisibility rules. It isn't an even number so it isn't divisible by 2. Since it ends in a 5—or a 0—we know it's divisible by 5. We divided the volume by 5 and got 25. Then all we had to do is check to make sure we could get 25 by multiplying 5 times 5, and we could! We knew that we had to find three numbers that were all the same to build a cube.

CORRIE: Nice thinking. What happened when you used this strategy to find the dimensions of a prism that is *not* a cube? Did it work?

STUDENT: It's not so easy. What we found out is that you can find *one* of the dimensions using divisibility rules. When you divide the volume by that number, what you get is the number of cubes in one of the layers. Then you have to try out some different combinations to find the dimensions of the layer.

STUDENT: But there's no guarantee that the first number you find is really one of the dimensions! Some volumes have *lots* of different prisms that work. So the best you can do is come up with a list of possible prisms with that volume.

Examples of Follow-up Assessment

Corrie gives her students one more day to extend their investigations of the volume of prisms. Then she gives them the following assignments:

■ Take one volume: 64 cubic units. List the dimensions of all possible rectangular prisms that can be built with that volume. Build or draw each prism to verify that its volume is 64 cubic units. How will you know you have found them all? Write about how you did your work and how you know you found all possible prisms with a volume of 64 cubic units.

■ Write about how you used division in your volume investigations. What did you know? What were you trying to find? Which numbers did you use? Why?

Several groups finish the assessment assignments early and are ready for another task. For these students, Corrie proposes the investigations *Hidden Hexahedra* and *Got You Covered!* (see Appendix H).

Reflecting on Selecting Meaningful Mathematical Experiences

As Corrie thinks about her students' comments during the class discussions, the quality of their work, and their engagement in the tasks she assigned, she feels encouraged. Never before had she seen the flicker of interest her students exhibited as they went about finding the volume of prisms. Most students want to continue their investigations with *Hidden Hexahedra* and *Got You Covered!* They make the following additions to the Volume Bulletin Board, providing further evidence of their engagement in the topic.

- We have a space for hay in our barn. How many bales of hay will fit in that space? How could the bales be arranged to give us the most hay in the least space?
- How many boxes will fit in the delivery truck?
- Which moving truck should we rent to move all our stuff?
- What is the smallest storage unit we can rent to hold our boxes?
- How many crushed cars will fit on a train car?
- Which boxes can we use for the 5,000-page print job? How many boxes will it take to hold the printing?

Corrie is pleased that her students have begun such an interesting list. Best of all are the positive parent phone calls she is starting to receive. Apparently, parents are also finding the mathematics she is teaching more interesting, and they are curious to see what else is being added to the list. Corrie decides to make the idea of real-life connections a regular feature of her math classes. She asks permission to set up a permanent display in an old trophy case in the front hall. Its title will be *Math in Our World*, and she will include various examples throughout the year of the real-world uses of the mathematics her students are learning. When some of the other grade levels ask if they can participate, Corrie's students say they will think about it! Right now, they want to see what fifth graders and their families can come up with to contribute.

Study Questions for Professional Learning Communities

1. Why is it important for teachers and students to find connections between the mathematics found within the four walls of a classroom and the broader world beyond?

2. How do you incorporate real-world contexts into lessons without losing the focus on the important mathematics?

3. When a student asks "Why do we have to learn this?" what kind of responses would make the math meaningful for them?

4. What are some ways you have made mathematics meaningful for your students?

5. Choose a topic that you have trouble motivating students to learn. How might you use a real-world context to make it meaningful for them?

Differentiating Instruction in a Focused Curriculum

A Lesson on Ratio and Rate

Eric is a thoughtful teacher who teaches in a school that draws from a widely varied population—from students whose parents are pouting because their kids did not qualify for accelerated mathematics to students who have no parental interest or support at all. Eric strives to differentiate his mathematics lessons in a way that provides varying levels of engagement in order for all of his students to be able to make purposeful connections to meaningful mathematics. He is not interested in providing instruction built around *neatsy-cutesy* enrichment tasks designed only to keep a few parents and students happy and then filling the remaining classroom time with basic drill and practice. He thinks it is important to focus his instruction on building depth of understanding in and connections among the critical ideas that will prepare *all* of his students for algebra in a few years. Experiences with new instructional strategies (such as the use of technology to provide differentiation opportunities) is causing him to revisit his thinking about how to maintain focus on the mathematics that all of his students must learn.

Planning for Focused Instruction

Lately, Eric has been hearing and reading numerous references to *algebra readiness*. Initially, he wasn't quite sure what it meant, so he did a little Internet research. In the long list of Algebra Readiness tests and resources he discovered, Eric saw that three topics appeared repeatedly: the basic operations, the understanding of fractions, and the ability to use simple expressions and equations. With a sigh, he thought, "Okay, I guess I just need to do *more* of all of these things," since his grade 6 district curriculum already included student learning objectives on whole number operations, addition and subtraction of fractions, and work with variables. However, as he continued to review some of the materials from his search, he also ran across the NCTM Curriculum Focal Point on ratio and rate in grade 6:

> *Number and Operations:* Connecting ratio and rate to multiplication and division   Students use simple reasoning about multiplication and division to solve ratio and rate problems (e.g., "If 5 items cost $3.75 and all items are the same price, then I can find the cost of 12 items by first dividing $3.75 by 5 to find out how much one item costs and then multiplying the cost of a single item by 12"). By viewing equivalent ratios and rates as deriving from, and extending, pairs of rows (or columns) in the multiplication table, and by analyzing simple drawings that indicate the relative sizes of quantities, students extend whole number multiplication and division to ratios and rates. Thus, they expand the repertoire of problems that they can solve by using multiplication and division, and they build on their understanding of fractions to understand ratios. Students solve a wide variety of problems involving ratios and rates. (2006, 18)

As Eric read this focal point, he realized that working with the idea of ratio in this way could include extra attention to multiplication and division, fractions, and expressions while strengthening his students' connections among these concepts and the concept of ratio. He wondered if this might be one way he could do more in the limited amount of time he has with each class. He thought that embedding practice with multiplication and division, fractions, and variables in the context of using ratios within a compelling problem-solving task might even make this work more interesting to his students.

Determining the Objective and Rationale for the Lesson

Eric has taught sixth grade in this district for several years. He knows that ratio is a concept that students first encounter in grade 6 in this district and that it is a difficult topic for most students to understand. As he plans his instruction on ratio, he reviews two of the student learning objectives in the district's mathematics curriculum for grade 6:

- The student is expected to use ratios to describe situations.
- The student is expected to use ratios to make predictions in proportional situations.

With the NCTM Curriculum Focal Points in mind, he also identifies five more student learning objectives in the district's curriculum that can be embedded and strengthened in the instruction he is planning on ratio:

- The student is expected to generate equivalent fractions.
- The student is expected to identify multiples of a given positive integer.
- The student is expected to use multiplication and division to solve problems.
- The student is expected to use a table to organize information.
- The student is expected to formulate equations from problem situations.

Eric decides to do an Internet search on *understanding ratio*. He finds an example of a visual of a tree that shows interrelated ideas in philosophy and creates a tree for himself about understanding ratio (Figure 9–1). In his tree he places whole number multiplication and division, multiples, and equivalent fractions in the roots, as ideas that support the growth of the understanding of ratio. Topics such as fractions, proportionality, similarity, probability, and measurement appear as connections to ratio.

Eric uses the branches and leaves of the tree to highlight the models, language, and symbols used to describe ratios in various settings. As he thinks about organizing these ideas into a meaningful experience, he considers what ratios are often used for in the real world—to describe scale models of toys or buildings or machinery or art. It strikes him that in order for there to be a sense of urgency for students to learn about the concept of ratio, it really needs to be related to a context, in a situation where using a correct ratio gives you a desirable result and using an incorrect ratio causes a problem.

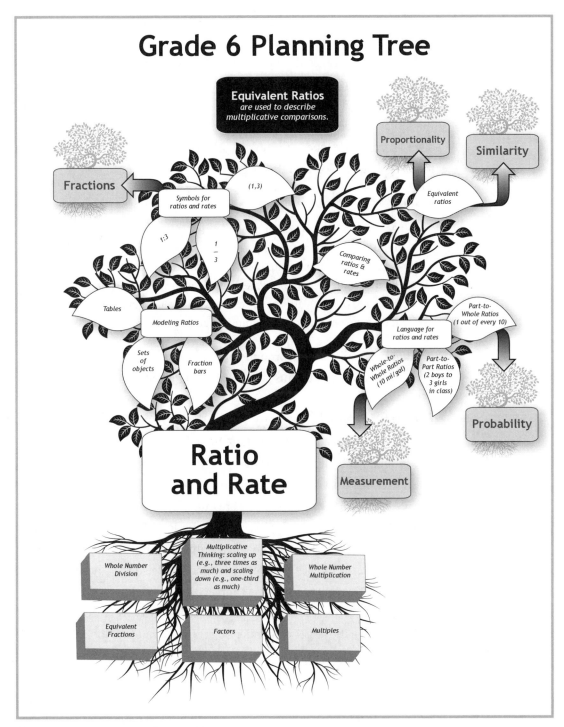

Grade 6 Planning Tree

Equivalent Ratios *are used to describe multiplicative comparisons.*

Proportionality

Similarity

Fractions

Symbols for ratios and rates

(1,3)

1:3

$\frac{1}{3}$

Equivalent ratios

Comparing ratios & rates

Tables

Modeling Ratios

Part-to-Whole Ratios (1 out of every 10)

Language for ratios and rates

Sets of objects

Fraction bars

Whole-to-Whole Ratios (10 mi/gal)

Part-to-Part Ratios (2 boys to 3 girls in class)

Probability

Ratio and Rate

Measurement

Whole Number Division

Multiplicative Thinking: scaling up (e.g., three times as much) and scaling down (e.g., one-third as much)

Whole Number Multiplication

Equivalent Fractions

Factors

Multiples

Figure 9–1 Grade 6 Planning Tree for Ratio and Rate

With that goal in mind, he identifies the following rationale for the lesson: Understanding the effects of maintaining a constant ratio between corresponding parts is the basis for understanding similarity and proportionality. Although the specific topics of similarity and proportionality don't appear in the grade 6 curriculum, he wants to include these ideas in his thinking as he designs instruction to prepare students to use ratios eventually to solve those types of problems. He identifies the following objectives for the grade 6 lesson on ratio:

The student understands that—

- A ratio is a comparison of two quantities.
- A ratio can compare two measurements.
- A ratio can be represented by a fraction.
- Equivalent ratios can be represented by equivalent fractions.
- To create objects with the same shape, you must maintain a constant ratio between the corresponding lengths of the two objects.

In addition, he plans to incorporate practice with applications of multiplication and division as students solve problems involving equivalent ratios.

Identifying an Engaging Task, Appropriate Materials, and Questioning Strategies

Eric's thinking about ratios and their relationship to scale models leads him to an idea for an engaging task. He is familiar with several books and movies that involve characters who are much larger or smaller than normal, such as *The Indian in the Cupboard* by Lynne Reid Banks (1980) and *Huge Harold* by Bill Peet (1961). He knows that his students are interested in the special effects in movies and television, so he decides to have them use equivalent ratios to build or draw simple, everyday objects for very small or very large characters. He likes the fact that this activity will incorporate self-checking, since the larger or smaller object they create will look right only if they find the correct measurements. They will have to multiply and divide accurately to create the ratios that translate the measurements of the normal-sized object to the measurements of the larger or smaller object. Since Eric wants his students to concentrate on the multiplicative patterns in equivalent ratios rather than just solve problems to find individual measurements, he designs a table (Figure 9–2) in which they can record their measurements in an organized way. (For the complete lesson plan, see Appendix I.)

Eric wants his students to be able to select the character and object that interests them. Although this leaves the activity very open-ended in that respect, he hopes that the ratio table will focus their attention on the mathematics. Eric also plans to ask the following questions at the end of the lesson to help students generalize the idea of equivalent ratios across the various situations:

- How did you use the ratio between the character and the normal-sized person to determine the measurements of your character's object?
- Did you use multiplication? If so, how?
- Did you use division? If so, how?
- Pick any pair of related measurements and divide one by the other. Now pick another pair of measurements and do the same thing. Do you get the same quotient? Why?
- What do you notice about your character's object? (It should look just the same, only smaller or larger.)
- Why do you think that happened?
- What do you think would happen if you changed the ratio in one of the pairs of related measurements?

Measurement of:					
Normal object					
Character's object					

Figure 9–2 Blank Ratio Table

Implementing the Focused Instruction

As Eric gathers the measuring tools for the activity, he decides to put out calculators as well. He wants students to understand when and why they are using multiplication and division in the activity, but he doesn't want any student to be unable to participate due to lack of fluency with certain computational procedures. The focus of this particular lesson is on the multiplicative patterns that occur in equivalent ratios and how equivalent ratios can be used to make shapes larger or smaller. Eric plans to note which students are having difficulty with the multiplication and division, suggest that they use calculators in this particular activity, and provide them with additional practice on computational procedures at another time.

Eric introduces the activity and models how students should use the ratio table for recording their measurements (Figure 9–3).

Eric points out that students must begin with some known relationship, or ratio—probably the relationship between their own height and the height of the character. Then, in order to keep the correct shapes of the objects, they will need to find measurements of appropriate parts of the normal object and determine the measurements of those parts of the character's object. Eric deliberately selects a beginning ratio that is a whole number multiple: sixty inches (as a representative height of a sixth grader) to ten inches. He models these two lengths with two measuring tapes, showing how it takes six of the shorter length to make the longer length. He introduces students to the language to describe ratios, saying, "Sixty-to-ten or six-to-one," and "I am six times as tall as the character; the character

Measurement of:	Height	Pencil	Length of table	Width of table	Height of table
Normal object	60 inches	6 inches	36 inches	22 inches	44 inches
Character's object	10 inches				

Figure 9–3   Ratio Table: Example 1

is one-sixth as tall as I am." He also connects symbols to the ratio language: *60:10; 6/1; 6 × 10 = 60; 60 ÷ 6 = 10.*

Eric then asks students to think about what would go in the ratio table for the other measurements of the character's objects, such as a pencil. He holds up six inches of the measuring tape as a model of the regular pencil's length and guides students to think about setting up the same relationship between the regular pencil's length and the new pencil's length.

ERIC: So, if you record 6 inches for the measurement of the regular pencil, how do you determine the measurement of the character's pencil?

STUDENT: You need to divide it by 6, like you did your height. That means a 1-inch pencil. That's a really little pencil!

ERIC: Well, yes, from our perspective. But from this smaller person's perspective, it would look just the same as ours, if we also made the other lengths just as small. Like with the table—we need to measure the length and width and height to make the whole table look right. What do we do to find the measurements of the smaller table?

STUDENT: Don't we need to do the same thing? Divide by 6? I can do 36 in my head and get 6 inches for the length of the table. But, the width and height aren't that easy.

ERIC: Any suggestions?

STUDENT: Just divide 22 by 6. You get 3 remainder 4.

ERIC: So, what does that mean for the measurement of the table? What do we do with the remainder?

STUDENT: We could just ignore it.

STUDENT: But wouldn't that be sort of like cutting off some of the table? I think we need to use all of the measurement.

ERIC: Remember how we continue division so that we don't have a remainder?

STUDENT: Oh, yeah. Make a fraction, like $3\frac{4}{6}$.

ERIC: So, if we had *ignored* the remainder, and just used 3 inches, then the length of our little table would be more than half an inch too short. That would make it look different to our character than our table looks to us.

Student: Can we use decimals? That is another kind of answer we get when we divide.

Eric: [Using overhead calculator] Let's see. If we enter 22 divided by 6 on the calculator, the answer displayed is 3.66667. Is that the same as or different from $3\frac{4}{6}$?

Student: I think it should be the same, because we did the same division. But it doesn't really look the same.

Eric takes a few minutes to do the division on the board to illustrate how the calculator display was created. He is glad that some students recognize intuitively that the quotients should be the same whether in fraction or decimal form. He writes a note to himself to revisit the discussion of decimal representations of thirds at another time, perhaps in this same context, after students feel more comfortable with the basic idea of equivalent ratios.

Eric then asks students to choose an object that they can draw or construct in a smaller or larger form, use the ratio table to determine the measurements of this object for their character, and draw or construct the object from the new measurements in order to see their results. The students may work by themselves or in pairs, but everyone has to make his or her own recording table to use during the questions at the end of the activity. He helps a few students decide on a character and an object, and everyone is soon hard at work, making and recording measurements.

Using Embedded Assessment to Support Focused Instruction

As Eric walks around the room, he begins to feel like a broken record. Although he made a list of possible questions that he could ask during the activity, he is mainly asking, "How would you change this measurement to the larger (or smaller) measurement? How do you know what to multiply (or divide) by?" But, he decides that since the focus of the activity is on the use of multiplication and division to create equivalent ratios, then it makes sense for him to be repeatedly asking these very focused questions.

Also, as he walks around the room, he sees students at very different levels of recognition of the constant multiplicative relationship between the pairs of numbers in their ratios. Some students have set up original ratios that are represented by decimals such as 2.8:1, or fractions such as 63/128:1. For students who are having difficulty seeing the multiplicative relationships, he simplifies the task by suggesting friendly numbers for their beginning ratios, such as 3:1 and 62:124. For students who are more comfortable with the multiplicative relationships and seem ready to work with more complicated numbers, he suggests the use of a calculator to do the multiplication and division involved in creating their ratio tables.

With fifteen minutes left in the class, the students have made several entries in their ratio tables but are not completely finished drawing and building their objects. Some of them are so intent on getting the details in their drawings *exact* that they keep erasing until they have holes in their papers. Eric decides that the class needs to stop and discuss some final questions to refocus their attention on the mathematical ideas before they leave.

Summary Discussion to Deepen Understandings

As he walked around the room during the activity, Eric identified three ratio tables that he thought would provide useful material for discussion. With the students' permission, he uses the document camera, which the district has just purchased, to display this work to the whole class.

> ERIC: If you want to spend time at home tonight finishing your character's object, please do so. Then you can put it in our class display tomorrow. Right now, I'd like you to think about some of the math that you used today and why. Let's look at this ratio table. [Eric shows the class Figure 9–4.] How would you describe this character's relationship to the student who did this table?
>
> STUDENTS: 55 inches to 11 inches; 55 to 11; 10 to 2; 5 to 1; 1/5.
>
> ERIC: I see all of those representations of the relationship in the table. We could summarize them all by saying, "The person is five times as tall as the character; or the ratio of the person to the character is 5 to 1." Or we can say that the character is 1/5 as tall as the person; the ratio of the character to the person is 1 to 5. I heard some of you using the word *inches* in your comparisons, but some of you didn't, and I didn't just now. In this situation, both ways are correct. We'll talk more about when we need units in ratios and when we don't.

Now, who would like to describe how this person used the numbers in the top row of the table to find the numbers in the bottom row of the table?

STUDENT: They divided by 5.

ERIC: Every time? I can see 55 divided by 5 is 11, and 10 divided by 5 is 2, and 5 divided by 5 is 1, but I was thinking that 1 divided by 5 would be 1/5. The number under 1 inch doesn't look like I expected one-fifth to look.

STUDENT: Well, that is what I got when I did 1 divided by 5 on the calculator.

ERIC: And how do you read this number?

STUDENT: Two-tenths.

ERIC: [Writing the fraction *2/10s* on the board] So the fraction *2 over 10* means the same as the decimal number *point 2*; they are different representations for the same number. And if we show this fraction in its simplest form? [Eric demonstrates the simplification of 2/10s to 1/5 on the board, a review of a previously encountered idea.] Then we see that this decimal [0.2] is also equivalent to 1/5.

At this point, Eric's head is spinning with all of the different questions about fractions, decimals, equivalences, and operations that he could ask. But time is getting short, and he wants to end with an opportunity for everyone to participate in some mathematics related to their work. So, he decides not to even look at the other two examples he collected from the class.

ERIC: Okay, let's use some symbols to record what we've learned about this ratio table. Let's use *x* to represent the numbers that we created

Measurement of:	Height	Length of book	Width of book	Thickness of book	
Normal object	55 inches	10 inches	5 inches	1 inch	
Character's object	11 inches	2 inches	1 inch	0.2 inch	

Figure 9–4   Ratio Table: Example 2

from actually measuring. [He writes this on the table being displayed to the class, as shown in Figure 9–5.] Anyone have any suggestions about how we might describe the numbers in the second row? How can we describe how each number in the second row was created from the number in the first row?

STUDENTS: We divided by 5. We used *x* divided by 5.

ERIC: So, we can represent *all* of the numbers that occur in the second row of this ratio table with the expression *x divided by 5.* [Eric writes the expression in the table as shown in Figure 9–6.] Your assignment for tomorrow is to figure out what expression you need to write for the second row of YOUR ratio table. Use *x* for the first row like we did on this one. Bring your ideas to class tomorrow, and we will discuss them.

As the bell rings, Eric returns the three ratio tables he borrowed. He is a little concerned that they had time to discuss only one example today. He is already planning to create a few examples of his own for tomorrow to make sure that

Measurement of:	Height	Length of book	Width of book	Thickness of book	
Normal object	55 inches	10 inches	5 inches	1 inch	*x*
Character's object	11 inches	2 inches	1 inch	0.2 inch	

Figure 9–5 Ratio Table: Example 3

Measurement of:	Height	Length of book	Width of book	Thickness of book	
Normal object	55 inches	10 inches	5 inches	1 inch	*x*
Character's object	11 inches	2 inches	1 inch	0.2 inch	$x \div 5$

Figure 9–6 Ratio Table: Example 4

the discussion will include expressions related to several different ratios and that everyone can be comparing the examples to his or her own table.

Examples of Follow-up Assessment

Although Eric's students aren't ready for a formal assessment yet on their understanding of ratio, he does think that he'd like to see if they can use a ratio table to display relationships in similar contexts. He decides that after they close their discussion on the current activity, he will ask them to choose one of the following three tasks to demonstrate their understanding of a ratio table:

1. A certain car can travel 240 miles on a 16-gallon tank of gas. Create a ratio table to determine how many miles the car can travel on 1 gallon, 2 gallons, 3 gallons, etc.
2. Create a ratio table and use it to make a scale drawing of yourself to fit on a 9 $\times$ 12-inch piece of manila paper.
3. If the statue of Abraham Lincoln in the Lincoln Memorial in Washington, DC, could stand up, it would be approximately 28 feet tall. Create a ratio table that tells you what the lengths of your feet, hands, arms, legs, and so forth would be if someone made a statue of you that was 28 feet tall.

Reflecting on Differentiating Focused Instruction

Although he had identified the understanding of ratio as the main objective of this lesson, Eric also knows that the concept of ratio is a complex understanding that must emerge from many experiences in many different contexts, and that will develop for different students at different times. He knows that his class will need to use ratio tables in a variety of problem-solving situations at different levels of difficulty that involve comparisons such as miles per gallon and cost per unit. He wants all of his students, no matter their facility with multiplication and division, to see the same models, hear the same language, and use the same symbols across these various situations to generalize the idea of equivalent ratios as multiplicative comparisons.

In addition, Eric knows from his previous years teaching sixth grade that, if he incorporates a variety of opportunities in his planning, there will be many chances for students to build this generalization. As one of his colleagues says, "Sixth grade is all about ratio." He just needs to make sure that his students recognize when and how the idea is being used, whether or not they are able to quickly do the computation involved.

As he waits for the next class, he jots down some notes about differentiating instruction to revisit as he plans. He considers how and when he might incorporate the use of spreadsheet software to help all students experience the power of the symbolic representations. For instance, they could replicate their own ratio tables by using the multiplication or division expression they identified for their table, no matter which numbers are involved. They could generate a whole new ratio table by changing the ratio used in their multiplication or division expression and make observations without getting sidetracked by incorrect computation. He wonders if this type of experience, in which technology does all the computation, can still contribute to students' understanding of ratio. As Eric leaves for the day, he is deep in thought about the issues of differentiating instruction within a focused curriculum in order to provide all students the opportunity to learn important mathematics.

Study Questions for Professional Learning Communities

1. How can you differentiate instruction and maintain mathematical focus?
2. What are some characteristics of a lesson that can provide opportunities for differentiated instruction?
3. If differentiation involves adapting instruction to students' needs, how can you make sure that it is equitable for all students? For example, if instruction is differentiated with the use of technology, can everyone get to do something interesting? Can everyone learn the important mathematics they need to learn?

4. Select a lesson that addresses an important mathematical idea at your grade level. From your knowledge and previous experiences, describe some difficulties that you think students might have in this lesson. Don't forget to include difficulties that might be exhibited by high-achieving students, such as an inability to describe their quick thinking.

5. Suggest some adaptations to the lesson that would address the difficulties identified in Question 4 and maintain the mathematical focus of the lesson.

Reflecting on Ways to Support Focused Instruction

Lessons Learned

Let's touch base with the teachers we have met in the pages of this book. In the following fictional scenario, we have asked the teachers to participate in a mathematics conference as part of a panel discussing the impact that teaching a focused mathematics curriculum has at the elementary level. We would like them to reflect on their experiences—particularly on the challenges, the excitements, the disappointments, the growth in their own professionalism, their knowledge of mathematics, and their understanding of how students learn important mathematics concepts. To begin, they will respond to the prompt: "I used to . . . but now I . . ."

Kindergarten: Anne

Anne starts the discussion: "*I used to* . . . allow my kindergartners to determine the direction a math lesson would take, based on their curious questions. I felt out of control. And at the end of the day—or week—or year—I was never sure what we had accomplished. I was never sure what evidence of understanding to look for because I didn't have a clear vision of where we were headed or the checkpoints we needed to make along the way. *But now I* . . . have a *plan*! I know exactly what my goal is for each student and what to look for and listen for as evidence of understanding. The focus I have achieved by prioritizing the big ideas we must address has given me the opportunity to keep a clear eye on the prize: student understanding of a complex web of mathematical concepts. The curious questions still come—as I want them to. But now we address the ones that don't directly relate to the focus of that lesson by writing them on sticky notes and attaching them to our "I wonder . . ." bulletin board. When time permits, we pull questions from the board and figure out together how to answer them.

"Another thing I have noticed this year is that my kindergartners have made much more progress creating number stories than ever before. Here are some number stories they came up with:

> As I looked out my bedroom window, I saw six butterflies. Four were yellow and two were orange.

> I helped my brother put pasta and meatballs on his plate. He wanted four meatballs and four pastas. That made eight pastas and meatballs on his plate.

> Last night I went outside with my dad, and we watched stars. We saw twelve stars. Ten were gold and two were silver. I can write that: $12 = 10 + 2$.

I think it is a direct result of using our work mats over and over again to conceptualize whole numbers in terms of two parts."

First Grade: Theresa

As a former fifth-grade teacher who now teaches first grade, Theresa reports: "*I used to . . .* point a finger at primary teachers and accuse them of concentrating on literacy at the expense of numeracy. *But now I . . . am* a primary teacher! Although literacy continues to take center stage in the primary classroom, I think I have convinced my colleagues to achieve an instructional balance between literacy and numeracy.

"One of my first-grade team's goals was to teach measurement all year long and to use measurement as a context for developing number sense. We concentrated on length and put up a bulletin board on which our children posted questions that could be answered by using nonstandard units to measure length. Here are some examples they came up with:

How much shorter is Danielle than David? (Units: linking cubes)

How deep is the fish tank? (Units: a string cut to size and then compared to small paper clips laid end to end)

How wide is the door of our classroom? (Units: craft sticks)

How far around is our reading table? (Units: a chain of large paper clips)

"We also estimated measurements for *everything* that sat still long enough: the number of Ping-Pong balls that will fill a cookie jar, and the number of marbles in the same jar; the number of drinking straws it takes to equal the length of the bookshelf, and the number of craft sticks it takes to equal the same length; the number of times children can write their first name in a minute, and the number of times they can write their last name in the same length of time. What I really like is that the children are now suggesting measurements they can estimate. Each time, we try to identify the unit we are considering as we estimate—such as the capacity of the cookie jar in *marbles* or the length of a minute in *first names*."

Second Grade: Dot

When her turn comes, Dot takes a deep breath and begins: "*I used to . . .* feel a lot of pressure from my district to cram third-grade content into what I considered to be an already full second-grade mathematics curriculum. *But now I . . .* am able to report on the impact our district's Vertical Team has had on our curriculum. We have established a mathematical focus for each grade level to enable teachers to make the best use of their instructional time. We still feel the pressure, but now we believe that teachers in grades three and beyond have a deeper appreciation of how far our young learners must come mathematically and the time it takes for them to do so.

"We chose Place Value as a focus for our second graders, and I must say we were pleasantly surprised when we began teaching addition and subtraction with regrouping—usually a real challenge for our children. We waited as long as we felt we could wait to give them time to develop facility partitioning two-digit numbers into standard and nonstandard groups of tens and ones. It just seemed like a natural progression into developing the meaning behind the standard algorithms we are required to teach in second grade. It was not exactly an *effortless* transition this year, but we have come a long way in a much shorter time than we have in years past."

Third Grade: Belinda

Belinda laughs as she begins to speak: "Well, as a brand-new teacher, I don't have much to tell. But I guess *I used to* . . . think of my students as a sea of expectant faces—all just waiting for me to impart important mathematical nuggets that would guarantee their future success. I must admit that I felt pretty confident. After all, I had graduated with honors from a major university with outstanding mathematics and education professors who really know about teaching and learning. *But now I* . . . see the sea of faces as individual children—each with unique needs. I quickly felt overwhelmed trying to master classroom management while also leading meaningful mathematical discussions. I realized that daily I was learning far more from my students than I could ever hope to teach them in a year. What helped me, though, was my team. Our district wanted us to focus on teaching multiplication and division, and I was able to contribute some ideas from my college classes. They made me feel like a valuable resource, and I will be forever grateful to them. My team decided to focus on different models for representing multiplication. We were able to create a long list of real-life reasons to multiply, complete with real-life examples of the models we were using. It was great!"

Fourth Grade: Gloria

By nature, Gloria is impulsive, eager, and a little nervous. She begins her part of the discussion by taking a deep, cleansing breath. "Okay! *I used to* . . . collect tons of activities, and I tried to use as many as possible. I thought that the key to keeping fourth graders tuned in was to keep them moving and involved. As a result, I nearly wore myself out rushing from one activity to another in my constant quest for more (and better) stuff for them to do! *But now I . . .* realize (thanks to Gwen, my math coach) that *more* is not always *better*! She has given me permission to calm down and focus on the key mathematical ideas my students really must learn. With the focus in front of me as a guide, I have learned to be more selective in choosing the perfect task for my students. My math coach has taught me that the most important gift I can give my fourth graders is quality time to dig deeply into important mathematical ideas. I feel I have time now to listen carefully to my students, to identify holes in their understanding, and to address those holes before moving on. Before, with so many busy activities, I couldn't see when important foundational ideas needed more attention. Our focus has also helped those classroom conversations stay on track instead of veering off and getting bogged down. I find it easier to manage fewer activities. I have less grading to do and more time to spend with my family! And I feel that my students have really benefited from our more relaxed classroom atmosphere."

Fifth Grade: Corrie

When Corrie's turn comes, she says, "I was so glad to hear Anne describe how focusing her math instruction allowed her to 'keep a clear eye on the prize.' In my case, I feel I changed what I thought of as the *prize*! *I used to . . .* trust my students' correct answers on reams of worksheets. I thought that those correct answers indicated mathematical understanding. *But now I . . .* realize they do not. I have discovered that the prize I am seeking is not necessarily evident in correct answers to low-level questions. Instead, I have learned to identify important big ideas in mathematics and to develop powerful questions to uncover the evidence of their emerging mathematical understanding.

"Motivation was also a big problem in my classroom. My students seemed to be dead inside. Focusing my mathematics instruction has allowed me to create within my classroom the culture of critical reasoning.

It now is coming closer to a place where kids can pose questions and test conjectures instead of merely memorizing and regurgitating unrelated information. I can't pretend that I have uncovered and filled all of the mathematical gaps that have developed over the years, but my students find math a lot more interesting. Some of them have confided that they are beginning to feel *smart*!

"I can also report that our efforts to make math more relevant have started to pay off. During our unit on volume, I asked students to bring in examples of situations where they might need to find volume. Several went home and interviewed members of their family. I actually received some positive comments from parents! That has never happened before!"

Sixth Grade: Eric

As Eric rises to speak, his quiet demeanor seems to belie the intensity behind his words. "*I used to* . . . feel a great conflict between the urgent needs of my lowest students and the longing of my highest students to keep learning new mathematics. I felt I had to either aim my instruction at my neediest at the expense of my brightest or vice versa. It seemed like a no-win situation! I also felt the looming pressure of having *all* of my students ready to learn algebra in just a few years. *But now I* . . . have discovered . . . Where do I begin?"

At this, Eric's reticence falls away completely. "When I began researching algebra readiness and the NCTM Focal Points for sixth grade, I had no idea how much mathematics I would learn! Do you know how many critical sixth-grade math concepts are embedded in proportionality? Tons! I was able to plan an investigation that had students paying extra attention to multiplication and division, fractions, and expressions while strengthening connections among these concepts and the concept of ratio. I think I finally see how I can accomplish a lot more in my limited class time. Another thing I discovered is how planning an open-ended investigation gave my gifted kids the challenge they were seeking while also providing my struggling students with an interesting context in which to build their skills and understandings. Our extension activity had students using a spreadsheet to play with variables and see immediately the impact on the relationships in their table. Man, we had fun!"

Eric, suddenly embarrassed, sits down. But the rest of the panel encourages him to stand with them to acknowledge the spontaneous applause from their audience.

The Big Picture

As a group, these teachers feel they have only started to uncover the complex comprehensions that make up the patterns and structure of the mathematics they hope to explore alongside their students. Each in his or her own way has made use of the tree as a model for the relationship between the prerequisite understandings (the roots), the emergent mathematical structure (the trunk), and the emerging complex understandings (the leaves and the branches). Each is finding ways to help his or her students make meaningful connections among the emerging understandings within a focused elementary mathematics curriculum. Each is developing an appreciation of curricular synergy in which the *whole* (a complex system of mathematical understandings) comes about as a result of the purposeful connections and interaction among the *parts* (the foundational concepts and skills).

In this book, we have suggested that an ever-changing, ever-evolving instructional environment can be considered a *complex system*, similar to an ecosystem. In some ways, the role of a teacher working within this educational ecosystem can be compared to the role of either a naturalist or an ecologist working within a biological ecosystem. A naturalist studying a forest will discover that it is composed of an almost infinite number of niches filled with organisms that eat, reproduce, nest, find protection, compete, and interact. By focusing on every single organism in isolation, a naturalist could never develop an understanding of the ecosystem as a whole. So, while a naturalist might appreciate the biodiversity in a forest, it takes an ecologist's synergistic thinking to thoroughly understand the forest as a complete ecosystem. It takes an ecologist to help us understand the impact that draining a wetland has upon migration patterns. It takes an ecologist to help us understand the impact that burning a rain forest in Brazil has upon global climate patterns. John Muir, the esteemed conservationist, described the interconnectedness of the natural world by saying, "When we try to pick out anything by itself we find that it is bound fast by a thousand invisible cords that cannot be broken, to everything in the universe" (Fox 1981, 291). The NCTM Curriculum Focal Points (2006) give us an *educational ecologist's* vision of mathematics. A teacher who takes on the role of ecologist within the complex system of the mathematics classroom, focusing instruction on the interactions among the parts, can help students make the connections needed to build the complex understandings that will prepare them for the mathematical challenges they will encounter in their futures.

Appendices

APPENDIX A   Planning Tree   ■   130

APPENDIX B   Lesson Plan Template   ■   131

APPENDIX C   Kindergarten Lesson Plan: Let's Make Five   ■   134

APPENDIX D   Grade 1 Lesson Plan: So *Now* How Long Is It?   ■   143

APPENDIX E   Grade 2 Lesson Plan: 100 or Bust!   ■   149

APPENDIX F   Grade 3 Lesson Plan: Modeling Multiplication   ■   158

APPENDIX G   Grade 4 Lesson Plan: Area: Why Multiply?   ■   168

APPENDIX H   Grade 5 Lesson Plan: Prisms from Cubes   ■   175

APPENDIX I   Grade 6 Lesson Plan: Just Right!   ■   183

Planning Tree

Figure A–1   Planning Tree   © 2010 by Jane F. Schielack and Dinah Chancellor from *Mathematics in Focus, K–6*. Portsmouth, NH: Heinemann.

Appendix B: Lesson Plan Template

TITLE of Learning Experience

Rationale and Objectives

A description of the conceptual mathematical idea(s) addressed in the lesson and how the concept(s) are important in building related complex mathematical understandings

The student understands the following:
A bulleted list of components that support the objective(s) of the lesson

Description of Lesson

A brief description of the task students will be engaged in

Materials

A list for preparing the lesson, including manipulatives, technology, literature, supplies

Procedure

Introduce

A description of how this lesson might be introduced to students:

- through a piece of literature
- through a provocative question *(What might happen if . . . ?)*
- through a previous experience

Are there prerequisite or scaffolding experiences that might be helpful for students?

Engage

A description of the task within the lesson and how it will engage students in learning the mathematics. Also, suggested ways during the lesson to incorporate embedded assessment to uncover evidences of understanding resulting from this learning experience. What questions might help students focus on the mathematics they are doing in the lesson? What mathematical language and symbols can you model related to the task and the objective? For embedded assessment, what do you want to look for and listen for as evidences of understanding? How can you focus students' attention on important patterns and encourage them to make inferences or generalizations related to the objective? How can you help students make and test conjectures related to the objective? What classroom management ideas might be used to support student engagement? (Working with partners or small groups? A suggested time frame for student engagement?)

Summarize

A list of some specific questions that are important to include in a summary discussion to focus students on what they have learned from the experience. The purposes of this summary discussion are to have students:

- share their problem-solving processes and solutions;
- compare solution strategies and look for different ways of approaching problems and describing solutions;
- uncover patterns or generalizations that may serve to connect this learning experience to important complex mathematical understandings; and
- analyze group dynamics (e.g., How did groups handle difficulties? How did they ensure that each group member could describe the process and solution?)

Follow-up Assessment Ideas

Suggested ways after the lesson to uncover evidences of understanding that have resulted from this learning experience. Could students respond to a writing prompt? (Make one up.) Could they perform a similar task that requires them to display their depth of understanding? (Describe the task.) Could they describe a reason to use the math concept(s) in the world outside of school? Could they create artwork, a song, a story, or a poem to display their depth of mathematical understanding?

Extension/Differentiation

Ideas for how this learning experience could be modified for different readiness or interest levels

Appendix C:
Kindergarten Lesson Plan

Let's Make Five

Rationale and Objectives

Conceptualizing whole numbers as sums of two or more addends builds flexible thinking and supports part/part/whole addition and subtraction strategies as well as partitioning numbers in sets of tens and ones, an important prerequisite for developing place value. Also, organizing work in a variety of ways provides a context for using patterns to make predictions and solve problems.

The student understands the following:

- Whole numbers can be represented by number combinations.
- Number combinations can be organized in a variety of ways.
- Depending on how number combinations are organized, different patterns emerge.
- Patterns can help to answer the question, "How do you know you have found all the ways to make a whole number in terms of its parts?"

Description of Lesson

Students will explore a variety of ways to represent the quantity *five* in terms of two parts using the fingers on both hands and using counters on work mats.

Materials

A variety of work mats and counters (Note: It is important that each scenario lend itself to representing the number five in terms of two parts.)

For Extension

Two-color counters, red and yellow crayons, cups, circle sheet, scissors (for cutting circle slips), chart paper or bulletin board for creating a class graph

Procedure

Introduce

- Pose the following question to the whole class: "How many different ways can you use the fingers on both hands to make *five*?"
- Ask students to organize themselves at the front of the room to show different ways they have found to make *five*.
- Discuss patterns they notice and how they can use those patterns to know when they have found all the ways to make *five*.

Engage

Set up each center with work mats for students to investigate and record how many different ways they can show *five* in terms of two parts, with zero as one possible part:

- leaves of two colors on a tree
- bears on two pieces of playground equipment—a sandbox and a slide
- two colors of ornaments on a tree
- ghosts and jack-o'-lanterns in a haunted house
- two colors of birthday candles on a cake
- frogs and toads in a pond
- boys and girls on a school bus
- rocks in two branches of a river
- airplanes on two runways
- silver and gold stars in the night sky
- red and blue balls juggled by a clown
- gold coins in two treasure chests
- yellow and orange butterflies in a garden

Direct students to work individually or in pairs. Ask them to visit a variety of centers, using the work mats and counters to build the quantity *five*.

For embedded assessment, circulate to ask questions as students work. Focus questions on the mathematical goals of the lesson—for students to fluently and flexibly compose and decompose numbers at least through the quantity *five*; to organize their work so they can look for patterns; and to use the patterns to solve problems and to answer important questions about their work. Look for the following evidences of understanding:

- Do the children effectively use principles of counting to build *five* with counters on work mats by using one-to-one correspondence; using an organized way of keeping track of objects being counted; showing that they know that the organization of the objects does not affect the total; and exhibiting cardinality/inclusion (the last number said equals the size of the group)?
- Does the child organize the work mats to show the variety of ways *five* was made? Listen for explanations of how children know they have counted *five* on each work mat and how each is a different way to make *five*. Also listen for descriptions of patterns in the combinations of numbers on the work mats.

Summarize

Include questions in a discussion at the end of the lesson to focus students' attention on what they have done and what they have learned from doing it:

- What work mats and counters did you use? Tell me some of the ways you made *five*.
- How did you organize your work? Did anyone choose a different way to organize their work?
- What patterns did you notice?
- How did you use those patterns to decide if you had found all the ways to make *five* in two parts?
- How did you work together during Center Time? Did any of you work with a partner? Did you share your materials? If you had problems, what did you do to work them out?

Follow-up Assessment Ideas

Use the *Hiding Assessment* activity to gather evidence that a child has conceptualized the quantity *five* in terms of two parts. Ask a child to give you five counters. Hide some counters under an opaque plastic bowl, show the rest, and ask, "How many are hiding under the bowl?" For example, if you show three counters and ask how many are under the bowl, the child will respond that there are two. Continue until you have randomly assessed all combinations of two numbers that make five.

Differentiation

- A child who accurately and confidently tells how many counters are hiding under the bowl is ready to work with a greater number. Send the child back to the center with a different target number.
- A child who is uncertain, makes several mistakes, or does not immediately name the number of missing counters needs further work with that quantity.

Extension: Let's Make . . . Five

Use the task card instructions to introduce children to the activity and have them use the circle slips as shown in Figures C–1 and C–2. Suppose the number five is chosen to work on. Children will spill five two-color counters and record by coloring five circles to match the spill. Each child will do this nine times. Help them organize the color slips into a class graph. After students work on the extension activity, discuss the following questions:

- What colors came up when you spilled the counters? How many different combinations did our class get with our spills? Do you think there might be other possible color combinations that we missed? Why or why not?
- How can you use numbers to describe the different spills we got?
- How might we organize the circle slips into groups? How should we arrange the groups to make a graph?
- What do you notice about our graph? What color combinations seemed to come up the most? The least?

Let's Make . . .

You need: circle slips, red crayons, yellow crayons, two-color counters, cup

■ Choose a number between 2 and 11. (Check with your teacher.)

■ Put that number of two-color counters in a cup.

■ Find the circle slips that match your number.

■ Spill your counters and color circles to show your spill.

■ Do this nine times.

■ Sort your circle slips into groups showing spills that are alike.

■ Put your circle slips where they belong on the class graph.

Figure C–1   Let's Make . . . Task Card

© 2010 by Jane F. Schielack and Dinah Chancellor from *Mathematics in Focus, K–6*. Portsmouth, NH: Heinemann.

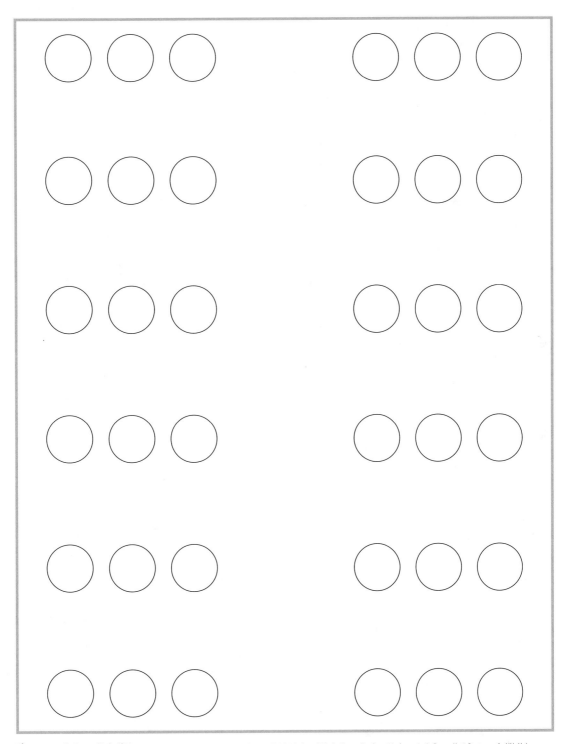

Figure   **C–2a**   Circle Slips   © 2010 by Jane F. Schielack and Dinah Chancellor from *Mathematics in Focus, K–6*. Portsmouth, NH: Heinemann.

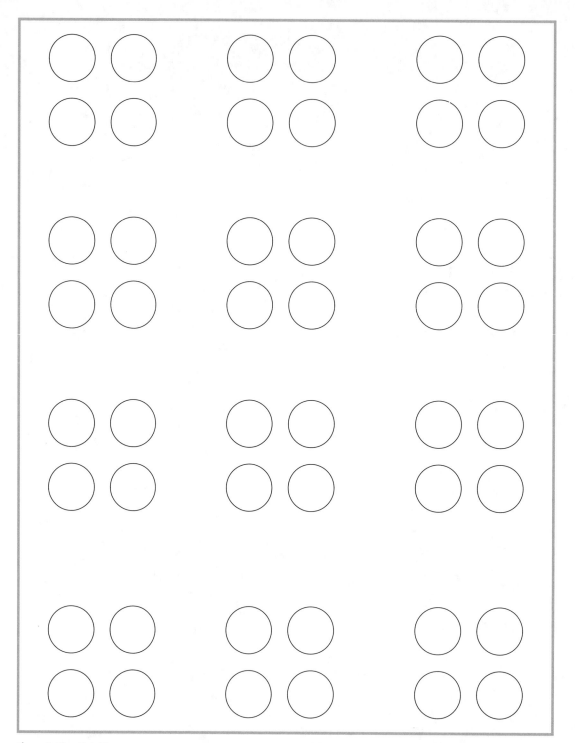

Figure C–2b Circle Slips

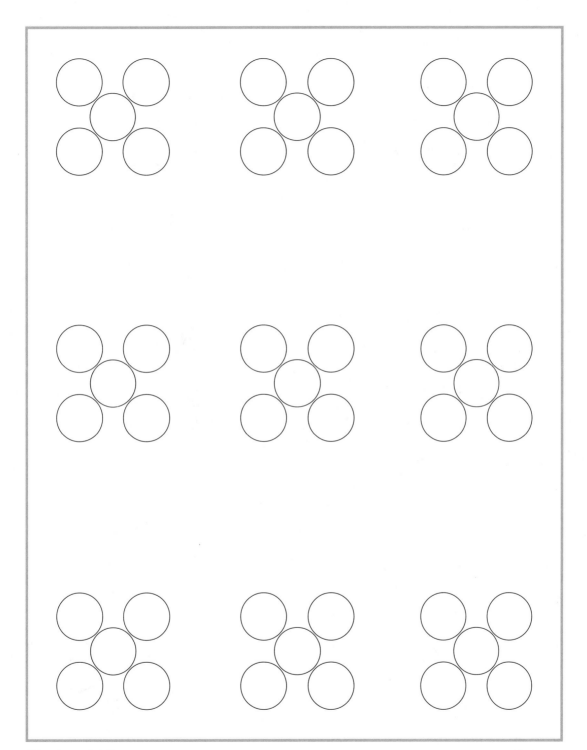

Figure C–2c   Circle Slips   © 2010 by Jane F. Schielack and Dinah Chancellor from *Mathematics in Focus, K–6*. Portsmouth, NH: Heinemann.

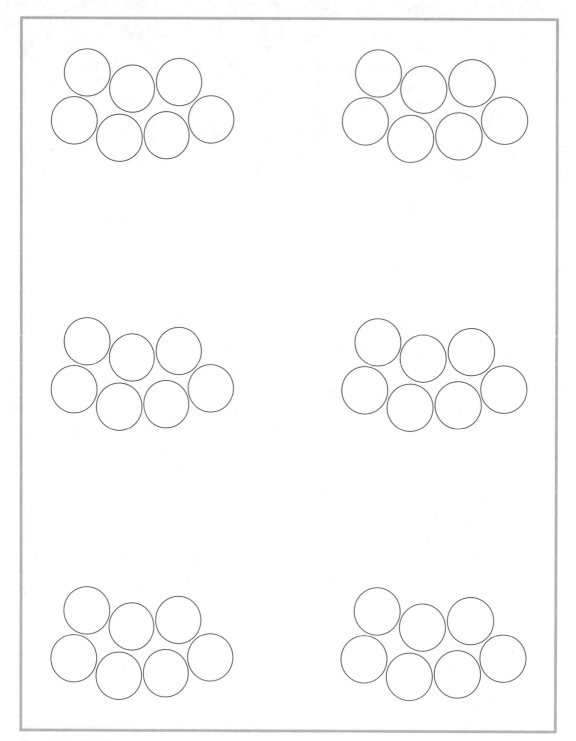

Figure C–2d Circle Slips

© 2010 by Jane F. Schielack and Dinah Chancellor from *Mathematics in Focus, K–6*. Portsmouth, NH: Heinemann.

Appendix D:
Grade 1 Lesson Plan

So <u>Now</u> How Long Is It?

Rationale and Objectives

Measurement involves concepts that are too complex to be mastered if children do not measure often and analytically. Measurement also gives students a reason to count and compare the results of measuring with different-sized units. Therefore, measurement provides a rich context for developing number sense.

The student understands the following:

- Length is an attribute that can be measured.
- Units of length must be uniform in size and must have the attribute of length.
- There is an inverse relationship between the length of a unit and the number needed to equal the length being measured.
- Skill must be used to compare units of length to an object being measured—no gaps, no overlaps.
- Estimation can be used to predict *about* how many units of length it will take to equal an object.

- Objects can be counted using a variety of different-sized groups without changing the total number of objects.
- To be skip-counted, groups must contain the same number of objects.
- Grouping by tens and ones is directly related to the notation used to record the number of objects.

Description of Lesson

Students will use two different nonstandard units to estimate and measure the length of a variety of objects/lengths/distances. They will group the units in a variety of ways to count them.

Materials

Nonstandard units of length (craft sticks, toothpicks, coffee stirrers, drinking straws, large paper clips, small paper clips, clothespins), twine, scissors

Estimation Stations

Station 1: small jar lid (such as from a baby food jar or a pimiento jar), lentils, unpopped popcorn, small paper cups (to group small objects to count them)

Station 2: medium-sized jar, snap cubes, centimeter unit cubes, small paper cups (to group small objects to count them)

Station 3: balance, classroom scissors, snap cubes, paper clips

Station 4: one-inch tiles, centimeter unit cubes, small paper rectangle (such as 3" × 5" index card), small paper cups (to group tiles/cubes to count them)

Station 5: plastic medicine bottle, pennies, lima beans, small paper cups (to group small objects to count them)

Station 6: snap cubes, lima beans, small paper cups (to group small objects to count them)

Procedure

Introduce

- Begin with a question that enables students to think about length in terms of a recognizable unit—the number of craft sticks it will take to equal the length of the chalk tray.

- Invite students to write their names on sticky notes and to place them on a class graph with labels "More than 25" and "Less than 25" to identify their estimates.

- Briefly discuss what they notice about the guesses they made.

- Give students a frame of reference by laying ten craft sticks end-to-end along the chalk tray. Allow students to use this information to refine their guesses and move their sticky notes if necessary.

- Ask a volunteer to continue to lay craft sticks end-to-end until they equal the length of the chalk tray. Discuss whether the craft sticks and the chalk tray come out exactly even.

- Then ask a student to count the sticks by ones. Write the total number of craft sticks and post it in a prominent place in the classroom.

- Next ask, "What if we were to group the sticks to count them? Do you think we will get the same total?" Invite students to respond to the question by describing the reasoning behind their answer.

- Ask students to verify their predictions by grouping the sticks in a variety of ways to count them.

- Ask, "What happens when we run out of groups of two (or five or ten) to count? How many did you get when you counted by twos? When you counted by fives? What about sets of tens? How many groups of tens did you make? How many extras? What is our total?"

- Refer to the total number of craft sticks posted where all could see it. Ask, "Did the number change when we grouped the sticks in different ways to count them? How can you explain this?"

- Refer to the number posted to show the total. Ask, "What did we write in the tens place? What about the ones place? Which way of grouping your sticks gave us results that are closest to the actual number we wrote to show the total?"

Engage

- Give pairs of students a craft stick and some toothpicks. Ask them to estimate the number of toothpicks it will take to equal the length of the chalkboard, discuss their ideas with their partner, and then record their estimate in crayon on a sticky note. Ask students to post their estimates on a class graph of toothpick estimates.

- Send pairs of students to the chalkboard to use toothpicks to verify their estimates. (*Embedded Assessment: Observe how students are using the toothpicks to measure the chalk tray. Are they laying them carefully end-to-end with no gaps and no overlaps?*) Ask students first to count the toothpicks by ones and record the total. Then ask them to put the toothpicks in equal groups (such as twos, fives, or tens) to count them, and then compare their totals with the results they got when they counted their toothpicks by ones. (*Embedded Assessment: Ask, "Do you think the total will change when you group the toothpicks by twos [fives, tens]? Why? What will you do when you run out of groups of twos [fives, tens] to count?" Note whether students realize that they are counting equal groups of toothpicks. Do they continue to count by twos, fives, or tens when they run out of equal groups to count? Or do they switch to counting by ones?*)

- Provide independent estimation tasks for pairs of students to work on while waiting for their turn to measure the chalk tray. At each station, students will record an estimate by choosing "More than _____" or "Less than _____"; group units to count them; and record the actual measurement. Students will then estimate using a different object/unit.

Estimation Stations

Station 1: How many lentils will fill the lid? How many kernels of popcorn will fill the lid?

Station 2: How many snap cubes will fill the jar? How many centimeter cubes will fill the jar?

Station 3: Using the balance scale, how many cubes will balance the scissors? How many paperclips will balance the scissors?

Station 4: How many tiles will cover the shape? How many centimeter cubes will cover the shape?

Station 5: How many pennies will fill the medicine bottle? How many lima beans will fill the medicine bottle?

Station 6: How many snap cubes can you grab with one hand? How many pinto beans can you grab with one hand?

Summarize

When all students have had a chance to record and post their estimates, use toothpicks to measure the chalk tray and group the toothpicks in a variety of ways to count them. Next, ask students to come to the front of the room for a summary discussion. Focus questions on:

- the reasoning behind their toothpick estimates;
- the graph of toothpick estimates;
- the total number of toothpicks it took to equal the chalk tray;
- whether the total changed when the toothpicks were grouped in a variety of ways to count them;
- which grouping method was directly related to the number used to record the total;
- what it means to measure length;
- the relationship between the length of the unit and the number needed to measure length;
- other things they could measure using craft sticks or toothpicks;
- other things that would make good units of length and why; and
- things that would *not* make good units of length and why.

Follow-up Assessment Ideas

Ask students to find at least one length (such as their height, the distance between their desk and the classroom door, the width of their desk, the length of a bookcase) by doing the following:

- estimating the number of craft sticks that will equal the length being measured (More than _____? or Less than _____?);
- recording the estimate;
- lining up craft sticks until they equal the length being measured;
- grouping the craft sticks by tens and extras to record the actual measurement;
- estimating the number of toothpicks to equal the same length;
- recording the estimate;
- lining up toothpicks until they equal the length being measured;

- grouping the toothpicks by tens and extras to record the actual measurement; and
- talking about what they discovered.

Extension/Differentiation

Provide a variety of supplies (such as ribbon or twine, linking cubes, paper clips, drinking straws, coffee stirrers, craft sticks, toothpicks, clothespins) and ask students to invent a way to measure something that is not straight (such as around the top of a trash can or the circumference of a watermelon, large pumpkin, or round table). Encourage students to try out their method and describe how well they think it worked.

Appendix E:
Grade 2 Lesson Plan

100 or Bust!*

Rationale and Objectives

Place value is a characteristic of our number system that allows us to be able to write infinitely many numbers with only ten digits. Students must develop the understanding that the value of a digit depends upon its position in a number in order to compare quantities and judge reasonableness of results.

The student understands the following:

- Numbers can be represented using a variety of models (a number line, base-ten blocks, calculators, and a place-value chart).
- Numbers can be partitioned into standard groups (tens and ones).
- The quantities represented by individual digits are determined by the position they hold in the numeral.
- The values of the positions increase in powers of ten from right to left.

Description of Lesson

Students will play a game in which they roll a die exactly seven times, each time placing the rolled digit in either the ones or tens column on a recording chart to generate a final sum as close to 100 as possible without going over.

---

*Texas Instruments activity used with permission.   149

They will analyze the game to see if a different decision each time they rolled the die could have resulted in a sum closer to 100 without going over it.

Materials (Per Group of Four)

Play money (one-dollar and ten-dollar bills), base-ten blocks (longs and units), hundred grid (10 cm $\times$ 10 cm), one die, calculator, meter stick (to serve as a number line), green triangle from pattern blocks, paper/pencil for creating a place-value chart on which to record decisions about where digits will be placed for each of the seven rolls of the die

Procedure
Introduce

- As a warm-up for the game, ask students to imagine that seven people have a total of exactly 100 dollars. Each person has either all one-dollar bills or all ten-dollar bills. How much money could each person have? Note: There are several possible answers.
- On the overhead projector, model the game by rolling the die, explaining the rules, demonstrating the four procedures/responsibilities, and recording the results on the recording sheet.

Procedures/Responsibilities

1. The first student rolls the die. Based on the whole group's decision, the student then records each of the resulting digits in the proper column on the place-value chart.
2. The second student uses base-ten blocks to represent the amounts on the hundred grid as they are written on the chart.
3. The third student uses the green triangle to point to the accumulating total on the meter stick.
4. The fourth student uses the calculator to keep a total by adding the amount of each roll of the die.

Rules:

- Roll the die exactly seven times.
- Write each digit rolled in either the ones or tens place (column) to make a sum that is less than or equal to 100.

Exactly $100

You need: play money ($1 bills and $10 bills), recording slips

▪ Seven people have exactly $100.

▪ Each person has either ALL $1 bills or ALL $10 bills.

▪ How much money could each person have?

▪ Write each solution on a separate recording slip.

How many different solutions do you think there are?

How can you organize your solutions?

What patterns do you notice?

How can you use the patterns to find more solutions?

Figure E–1   Task Card for the Warm-up   © 2010 by Jane F. Schielack and Dinah Chancellor from *Mathematics in Focus, K–6*. Portsmouth, NH: Heinemann.

Exactly $100	
Person	Amount
1	
2	
3	
4	
5	
6	
7	
Total	$100

Exactly $100	
Person	Amount
1	
2	
3	
4	
5	
6	
7	
Total	$100

Exactly $100	
Person	Amount
1	
2	
3	
4	
5	
6	
7	
Total	$100

Exactly $100	
Person	Amount
1	
2	
3	
4	
5	
6	
7	
Total	$100

Exactly $100	
Person	Amount
1	
2	
3	
4	
5	
6	
7	
Total	$100

Exactly $100	
Person	Amount
1	
2	
3	
4	
5	
6	
7	
Total	$100

Exactly $100	
Person	Amount
1	
2	
3	
4	
5	
6	
7	
Total	$100

Exactly $100	
Person	Amount
1	
2	
3	
4	
5	
6	
7	
Total	$100

Exactly $100	
Person	Amount
1	
2	
3	
4	
5	
6	
7	
Total	$100

Figure E–2   Recording Sheet for the Warm-up   © 2010 by Jane F. Schielack and Dinah Chancellor from *Mathematics in Focus, K–6*. Portsmouth, NH: Heinemann.

100 or Bust!

Rules:

■ Roll a die exactly seven times.

■ Write each digit rolled in either the ones or tens column to make a sum that is less than or equal to 100.

Responsibilities:

1st Student: Rolls the die and writes each of the resulting digits in the correct column on the place-value chart.

2nd Student: Uses base-ten blocks to show the amounts on the hundred grid as they are written on the chart.

3rd Student: Uses the green triangle to point to the accumulating total on the meter stick.

4th Student: Uses the calculator to keep a total by adding the amount of each roll of the die.

Figure E–3   Rules and Responsibilities of 100 or Bust!

© 2010 by Jane F. Schielack and Dinah Chancellor from *Mathematics in Focus, K–6*. Portsmouth, NH: Heinemann. (Texas Instruments activity adapted with permission.)

100 or Bust! Recording Sheet

Place Value Charts

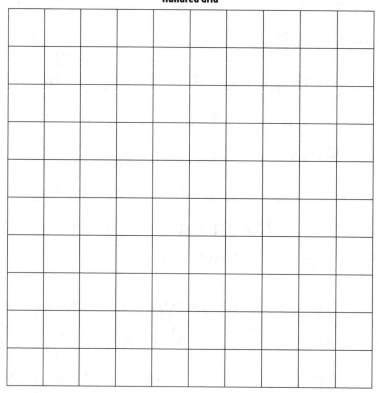

Game 1	Tens	Ones
1		
2		
3		
4		
5		
6		
7		

Game 2	Tens	Ones
1		
2		
3		
4		
5		
6		
7		

Game 3	Tens	Ones
1		
2		
3		
4		
5		
6		
7		

Hundred Grid

Strategies we used while we were doing this activity:

Figure E–4   Recording Sheet for 100 or Bust!   © 2010 by Jane F. Schielack and Dinah Chancellor from *Mathematics in Focus, K–6*. Portsmouth, NH: Heinemann.

Example: The first student rolls a 3. The group decides to put the 3 in the tens column. The first student writes 3 in the tens column and 0 in the ones column. The second student uses base-ten blocks to represent 30 on the hundred chart, as shown in Figure E–5. The third student uses the green triangle to point to the 30 on the number line represented by the meter stick, as shown in Figure E–6. The fourth student enters 30 in the calculator.

Engage

Have students play the game at least four times, rotating the responsibilities each time, so that each student gets to work with each representation. Remind students that each time they play, they should look for strategies to play a better game.

Ask students the following questions as they do the activity to focus attention on the mathematics:

- What information does the place-value chart give you that the other three don't?
- What do the base-ten blocks on the hundred grid show that the calculator and place-value chart don't?

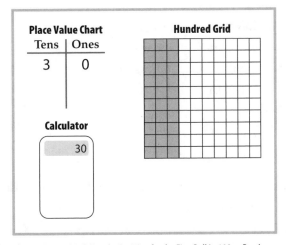

Figure E–5   Modeling the Decision for the First Roll in 100 or Bust!

Figure E–6   Modeling on the 0–100 Number Line

- What does the number line help you do?
- What does the calculator help you do?
- What do you do if your models don't match one another?

Summarize

Include the following types of questions in a summary discussion:

- Why did most people place their first numbers in the tens place?
- How did you decide where to put the small numbers you rolled?
- How did you use the information from the models to make your decisions?

Follow-up Assessment Ideas

Questions/Tasks to Uncover Evidence of Understanding

- Ask students to rearrange the digits in the games on their place-value charts to see if they can get closer to 100 without going over.
- Encourage students to make up a game that would reach exactly 100 in seven rolls of a die. Ask:

  - How many different ways can you do this?
  - How could you organize the ways you found to do this?
  - Do you see a pattern in the ways you found?
  - How can you use the pattern(s) to tell if you have found all the ways to reach exactly 100 in seven rolls?

Extension/Differentiation

Ask students the following questions:

- How would the game change if you used a ten-sided die or a spinner with digits zero through nine? Try it to see.
- How would the game change if you could go over 100, or if you could choose to add or subtract? Could you get closer to 100? Find out.

For students who would benefit from more opportunities to work with numbers they group in a variety of ways to count—including tens and extras—give them collections of objects to estimate and then have them use skip counting to find actual quantities. A task card for this activity is in Figure E–7.

How Many?

You need: large jar filled with snap cubes

■ How many cubes do you think are in the jar?

■ Use a crayon to write your estimate on a sticky note.

■ Count to find out.

What if you group the cubes to count them? Will your total change? Find out!

■ Snap your cubes into sets of five and extras. How many are there now?

■ Snap your cubes into sets of ten and extras. How many are there now?

*What did you do when you ran out of sets of **five** to count? Were there extras? How did you count them?*

*What did you do when you ran out of sets of **ten** to count? Were there extras? How did you count them?*

Figure E–7   Task Card for Counting with Groups   © 2010 by Jane F. Schielack and Dinah Chancellor from *Mathematics in Focus, K–6*. Portsmouth, NH: Heinemann.

Appendix F:
Grade 3 Lesson Plan

Modeling Multiplication

Rationale and Objectives

Fluency with multiplication goes well beyond the ability to remember basic facts. Having access to a variety of models for multiplication and making connections among them strengthens students' fluency.

The student understands the following:

- Whole number multiplication can be represented using a variety of models (e.g., joining equal groups, equal jumps on a number line, repeated addition, skip counting, arrays, area of a rectangle).
- Each of these models can be represented mathematically with a multiplication equation consisting of one factor that describes the number of groups, one factor that describes the number in each group, and a product that describes the total.
- A *word problem* situation that fits one of the models of multiplication can be described as "___ groups of ___" and can be represented by and solved using a multiplication equation.

Description of Lesson

Students will represent a given multiplication situation in a variety of ways: as joining equal groups, as equal jumps on a number line, as a repeated addition equation, as an array, and as a multiplication equation. They will

identify what is common about the representations and use the language
"_____ groups of _____."

Materials (Per Pair of Students)

One six-sided die, one-inch color tiles in at least two colors, crayons, laminated number line (or ruler) with one-inch units, dry erase marker, paper, pencil

Procedure

Introduce

■ Ask students to generate lists of *things that come in groups*—such as eyes (twos), corners on a triangle (threes), tires on a car (fours), number of pennies in a nickel (fives), and so forth. (See directions on Figure F–1.)

■ Record ideas on separate charts with titles such as *Things that Come in Threes* and post. Invite students to add to the lists as ideas occur to them.

■ Use the structured recording sheet (Figure F–2) to model with the students the following actions and dialogue you want them to practice in their pairs:

1. Choose an idea from one of the lists and use the color tiles to represent the equal groups. For example, you would represent wheels on a tricycle with groups of three tiles.

2. Roll the die to tell you how many of those *groups* you have. For instance, rolling a 4 means you have *four tricycles*, or *four groups of three wheels*.

3. Use the color tiles to show the four groups of three and say, "We have four groups of three." [Note: One student in a pair could do this step, and the other student in the pair could do Step 4. If possible, have students use at least two different colors of tiles. The students should make each group of tiles be one color, alternating colors between groups, e.g., making a group of three red tiles, a group of three blue tiles, a group of three red tiles, and a group of three blue tiles.]

Modeling Multiplication A

You need: color tiles (two colors), laminated number line, dry erase marker, die, recording sheet, crayons

■ Choose an idea from the list of things that come in threes (such as wheels on a tricycle). Write what you are counting.

■ Roll the die and use piles of tiles to show that number of groups.

■ Line up the tiles above the number line using alternating colors. Use the marker to show the groups as jumps on your number line. Use crayons to transfer to your recording sheet.

■ Rearrange the groups of tiles to make an array alternating colors in each column. Color the grid on the recording sheet to match your array.

■ Use words and numbers to describe the equal groups.

Figure F–1 Task Card for Modeling Multiplication A

© 2010 by Jane F. Schielack and Dinah Chancellor from *Mathematics in Focus, K–6*. Portsmouth, NH: Heinemann.

Modeling Multiplication A

We are counting _____

Number Line

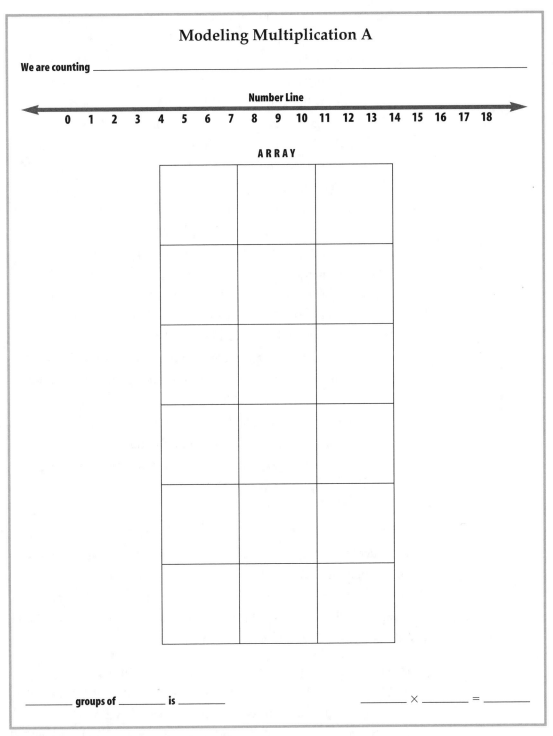

0 1 2 3 4 5 6 7 8 9 10 11 12 13 14 15 16 17 18

ARRAY

_____ **groups of** _____ **is** _____   _____ × _____ = _____

Figure F–2   Recording Sheet for Modeling Multiplication A

© 2010 by Jane F. Schielack and Dinah Chancellor from *Mathematics in Focus, K–6*. Portsmouth, NH: Heinemann.

4. Now show the four groups of three on the number line by drawing equal jumps from 0 to 3 (three units), 3 to 6 (three units), and 6 to 9 (three units). [Note: Students will be familiar with representations on number lines from their work in earlier grades with addition and subtraction.]

5. Work together to match the groups of tiles to the jumps on the number line. [Note: Since the tiles are one inch and the units on the number line are one inch, the tiles should form a solid bar. Having students use two colors of tiles will allow the students to make adjacent jumps different colors, so that they can still see the separate groups of three tiles.]

6. Then rearrange the tiles on the number line into an array, with each equal group forming a row of the array. [Note: In this example, there would be four rows of three, to represent the four jumps on the number line—that is, the four groups of three wheels. The array can be displayed with *space* between the tiles, or, with square tiles, the tiles can be *pushed together* to look like a rectangle. Again, having students use two alternating colors of tiles for each row in the array will allow students to still see the individual groups of three.]

7. Finally, write the appropriate multiplication equation (e.g., $4 \times 3 = 12$) to go with your situation and practice reading it. For example, "Four groups of three equal twelve."

Engage

Have students use the open-ended recording sheet (Figures F–3 and F–4) to go through this cycle at least three times while you circle the room. Watch and listen for misconceptions or the need for more guidance. Ask students the following questions as embedded assessment as they do the activity to focus their attention on the mathematics:

■ How many groups of tiles do you have? How many are in each group?

■ How did you show that on the number line? Where do you see the groups? Where do you see how many are in each group?

■ How are your groups of tiles and your jumps on the number line alike?

Modeling Multiplication B

You need: color tiles (two colors), laminated number line, dry erase marker, die, recording sheet, crayons

- ■ Choose an idea from the list of things that come in groups (such as feet on a cat). Write the groups you are counting.

- ■ Roll the die and use piles of tiles to show that number of groups.

- ■ Line up the tiles above the number line using alternating colors. Use the marker to show the groups as jumps on your number line. Draw your number line on the recording sheet.

- ■ Rearrange the groups of tiles to make an array, alternating colors in each row. Draw and color a grid on the recording sheet to show your array.

- ■ Use a sentence and an equation to describe the equal groups.

Figure F–3   Task Card for Modeling Multiplication B

Modeling Multiplication B

We are counting _____

Number Line

←——————————————————————————————————————→

A R R A Y

Sentence: **Equation:**

Figure F–4   Recording Sheet for Modeling Multiplication B

- What does your array look like? Where do you see the groups? Where do you see how many are in each group?
- How is your array like jumps on the number line?
- How is it like your beginning groups of tiles?
- What multiplication equation did you write? Where do you see the number of groups? Where do you see how many are in each group?
- What other things have you noticed about multiplication?

Summarize

Include these types of questions in a summary discussion:

- What does 2 × 3 mean? 4 × 6? Can you describe these in pictures? In words?
- When do we use multiplication?
- Make up a question for which you could use multiplication to find the answer.

Follow-up Assessment Ideas

Use these questions and tasks to uncover evidence of understanding:

- Ask a group of students to show you one of their multiplication situations on the recording sheet and explain what they did. Watch for their comfort levels in connecting the equal groups of tiles to the jumps on the number line to the rows and columns in the array.
- Give students one or two word problems involving a multiplication situation and have them select and record a representation to use to solve it.
- Give students a set of word problems that include a few that can be solved using multiplication and a few that cannot (involving unequal groups). Have them circle the problems that can be solved using multiplication.

Extension/Differentiation

Since these representations and connections are basic understandings about multiplication needed by everyone, differentiation will exist in the amount of time each student needs to work with the models. Students who grasp the basic concept of multiplication quickly can work on the activity *Author! Author!* (Figure F–5).

Use these extension questions to help students begin forming connections to division:

- If we know the total number of tiles and the size of each group we have, can we figure out how many groups we have? If so, how?
- If we know the total number of tiles and the number of groups we have, can we figure out how many tiles are in each group? If so, how?
- If we know only the total number of tiles we have, can we know for sure how many groups and the size of the groups we started with? Why or why not?

Author! Author!

You need: models for multiplication and division (color tiles, cm cubes, grid paper, number line) drawing paper, crayons/markers

■ Choose a model (such as an array).

■ Invent a real-life situation it could represent (such as cans of dog food in a case).

■ Write one or two original multiplication or division problems to go with your situation.

Here are some examples:

1. Mark is buying a case of dog food that comes in six rows of four cans. How many cans are in the case?

2. Mark is going on a trip for a week and his neighbor will feed his dog, Shadow. He gives him a whole case of dog food (six rows of four cans). If Shadow eats two cans of food every day, did Mark buy enough dog food?

■ Illustrate your problem and post it for your classmates to solve.

Figure F–5   Task Card for Author! Author!   © 2010 by Jane F. Schielack and Dinah Chancellor from *Mathematics in Focus, K–6*. Portsmouth, NH: Heinemann.

Appendix G:
Grade 4 Lesson Plan

Area: Why Multiply?

Rationale and Objectives

Students in grade 5 and above often confuse the formulas for calculating perimeter, area, and volume. So, before using these formulas, fourth graders need to build their knowledge of the actual attributes being measured (e.g., perimeter as a type of length and area as the amount of surface covered), and how these attributes are reflected in the various formulas. Specific experiences that compare and contrast measures of perimeter and area can strengthen the understanding of both attributes and the computational procedures related to each of them.

The student understands the following:

- Area is an attribute that can be measured.
- Units of area must be uniform in size and have the attribute of area.
- Area can be measured more accurately with units of area that are shaped like squares, because they fit together easily into rows and columns and the squares can then be counted using multiplication.
- Every two-dimensional shape has a perimeter (the distance around) that is measured with linear units and area (the amount of surface covered) that is measured with square units.

- The perimeter of a rectangle can be computed by adding together all of the lengths of the sides of the rectangle. This sum tells you how many linear units it takes to outline the shape.
- The number of square units of area in a rectangle can be computed by multiplying the linear dimensions of the rectangle. These dimensions tell you how many rows and columns of squares it takes to cover the rectangle.

Materials

Grid paper (cm or inch), scissors, markers, and tiles

Description of Lesson

Students will use grid paper to create rectangles whose perimeters are twenty-four units. They will determine the area of each rectangle and explore patterns between the dimensions of the rectangles and the areas of the rectangles in order to understand the procedure of multiplying length times width to find the area of a rectangle.

Procedure

Introduce

- Present a real-life context for the problem (Figure G–1). For example, "Our class has twenty-four meters of edging to put around the rectangular vegetable garden that we are going to make outside. In terms of area, what size vegetable garden can we make?"
- Have students review the characteristics of a rectangle.
- Review the attribute of perimeter as the length around a shape.
- Introduce the attribute of area, the surface covered by a shape. Introduce the square unit as the standard type of unit for measuring area, since they are *pieces of area* and can be fit together easily into rows and columns.
- Model how square tiles can be used to cover a shape with as few gaps and overlaps as possible and then be counted to estimate the area of the shape.
- Have students compare and contrast measuring the perimeter of a shape (using a unit of length) and measuring the area of a shape (using a square unit of area).

Rectangular Gardens

You need: grid paper, scissors, markers, tiles

■ Find as many rectangles as you can that have a *perimeter* of 24 units.

■ Cut out your rectangles. Record the *area* on each rectangle. (Remember to also write the unit of area.)

■ Record the length, width, and area of each rectangle in the table.

■ Write about any patterns you observe.

Figure G–1   Task Card for Rectangular Gardens

© 2010 by Jane F. Schielack and Dinah Chancellor from *Mathematics in Focus, K–6*. Portsmouth, NH: Heinemann.

- Have students talk about and show (perhaps on an overhead screen) how they can model the problem by using square tiles and grid paper to represent a rectangular garden with a perimeter of twenty-four units.

- For one of the rectangular gardens modeled, have students identify the dimensions of the rectangle, length and width. (Note that it is important to recognize that either dimension of the rectangle can be length or width. The mathematically important point is that there will be two linear dimensions multiplied together to make a *square* dimension that represents area.)

- Model for students how to record the two dimensions of each rectangle they make, length and width, and that rectangle's area on the recording sheet for discussion later (Figure G–2).

Explore

Have students work in groups of three or four to create as many models as they can of possible rectangular gardens with perimeters of twenty-four units. As you observe them working, ask the following questions to focus their attention on the objectives of the activity:

- What is the perimeter of the rectangle? How do you know?
- What part of the grid or tiles do you count to determine the perimeter?
- What is the area of the rectangle? How do you know?
- What part of the grid or tiles do you count to determine the area?
- What part of the grid or tiles tells you the length and width of the rectangle? How do those relate to the perimeter?
- What relationship do you notice in your table between the length and width of the rectangle and the number of squares in, or area of, the rectangle?

Note that using the tiles and the grid will cause most students to limit their exploration to whole number dimensions. However, if students are curious about fractional dimensions (e.g., a rectangle that measures $9\frac{1}{2}$ units by $2\frac{1}{2}$ units), they can use the grid to draw a rectangle with these dimensions and then join parts of squares into whole squares to determine the area.

Recording Sheet for Rectangular Gardens

Length	Width	Area

What relationship do you see between the dimensions of a rectangle and its area?

Test your observation with some different rectangles.

Figure G–2 Recording Sheet for Rectangular Gardens

© 2010 by Jane F. Schielack and Dinah Chancellor from *Mathematics in Focus, K–6*. Portsmouth, NH: Heinemann.

Summarize

In the summary, have students share the data in their tables. Record it in a common table for the whole class to see. Discuss if organizing the data in some way would help in making observations. Students may want to put the rectangles in order by area, or they may want to organize them by increasing length (which they will then notice causes decreasing width). Focus students' attention on the relationship of rectangular area to multiplication by asking questions such as:

- What does the length of a rectangle describe about the squares covering it? (How many objects in each row)
- What does the width of a rectangle describe about the squares covering it? (How many rows)
- What do the squares covering the rectangle measure?
- How do the squares covering the rectangle compare to an array (an arrangement that has a given number of equal rows of objects)?
- How do we use multiplication to count the number of objects in an array?
- Is it true in our examples that length times width of the rectangle is equal to the number of squares covering the rectangle? How is this related to the area of the rectangle?
- Does it make sense mathematically that we multiply the length times the width of a rectangle to find its area?
- How do we write the area of the rectangle so that we know that it is a measurement describing area? (With the label of square centimeters, or square inches, or square feet)

Follow-Up Assessment Ideas

Offer students the following challenges:

1. Given rectangles with the following dimensions, use multiplication to predict what you think the area of each rectangle will be. Then test your prediction using tiles or grid paper.

   a. 13 cm by 5 cm   b. 10 cm by 10 cm   c. 24 cm by 3 cm

2. If a rectangle has an area of thirty-six square inches, what could its length and width be?

3. If a rectangle has an area of fifty-six square inches and its length is 8 inches, what is its width?

Extension/Differentiation

■ Use grid paper to explore what happens when the dimensions of a rectangle are not whole numbers.

■ Given a parallelogram, can you rearrange its area so that it is a rectangle? How does that affect its area? How is the area of the new rectangle related to the area of the original parallelogram?

■ Given two triangles that are the same size and shape, can you arrange their areas into a rectangle? How does that affect their area? How is the area of the new rectangle related to the area of one of the original triangles?

Appendix H:
Grade 5 Lesson Plan

Prisms from Cubes

Rationale and Objectives

Measuring volume requires an understanding of the properties of polyhedral solids, especially rectangular prisms including cubes. It also provides a rich context for using the operations of multiplication and division.

The student understands the following:

- Volume is a measurable attribute of three-dimensional space.
- A cube is the standard unit of volume because it takes up three-dimensional space. Cubes must also be uniform in size.
- Surface area is the two-dimensional outside covering of a three-dimensional object.
- A square is the standard unit for measuring surface area because it is also two-dimensional.
- Skill must be used to compare units of volume/area to an object being measured—no gaps, no overlaps.
- Estimation can be used to predict *about* how many units of volume it will take to fill a box or to build a rectangular prism with interlocking cubes.

- Although units can be iterated and counted to find volume, the operations of multiplication and division provide more efficient strategies.

Description of Lesson

Students will use cubic units to estimate and find the volume of a variety of rectangular prisms. They will organize their work to look for patterns and make generalizations. Students will analyze how multiplication and division can be used in investigations involving volume. In a follow-up lesson, students will investigate how volume and surface area change as dimensions change.

Materials

Interlocking cubes; task cards/transparencies/handouts—Task Card for Prisms from Cubes, isometric dot paper, Hidden Hexahedra, Got You Covered!; chart paper and markers for each group

Procedure

Introduce

- Briefly review the differences between linear measure, area, and volume.
- Ask students to brainstorm attributes of a rectangular prism.
- Clarify the attributes of a cube as a *special rectangular prism*.
- Ask students to hold up one linking cube. Then describe its dimensions: "It is one unit high, one unit wide, and one unit long, or one by one by one. It takes one cube to build it, so it has a volume of one cubic unit."

Engage

Ask students to follow the directions on the Task Card for Prisms from Cubes (Figure H–1). Ask students to save the prisms they make during the activity to use for further investigations. Or if there is a limit to the number of available cubes, ask students to draw pictures of them on isometric dot paper (Figure H–2). With students, look for patterns in the chart data and have them use the patterns to make conjectures about finding the volume of any rectangular prism. For embedded assessment, as students work, ask questions such as:

Prisms from Cubes

- Use interlocking cubes to build a variety of rectangular prisms.

- For each one, record:

  - the dimensions of your prism (e.g., 2 × 3 × 4)

  - the number of cubes it took to build it by drawing a picture on the dot paper

- Organize your data into a chart.

- Describe the patterns you see in your data.

- If you know the dimensions of your prism, can you figure out how many cubes it takes to build it? Explain.

- If you know the volume of a prism, can you figure out its dimensions? Explain.

Figure H–1   Task Card for Prisms from Cubes   © 2010 by Jane F. Schielack and Dinah Chancellor from *Mathematics in Focus, K–6*. Portsmouth, NH: Heinemann.

Figure H–2   Isometric Dot Paper

- How are you figuring out the volume of each of your prisms? Are you counting the cubes or did you come up with a shortcut?
- You are building a big prism. What will you do if you run out of cubes?
- How are you organizing your data to create your chart? What patterns seem to be emerging?

Summarize

Ask students:

- How many different prisms did you build? How did you know each was different?
- Did you have enough interlocking cubes to build each of your prisms? If you ran out, how did you handle this?
- How are you using the operations of multiplication or division to find volume? What do you know? What are you trying to find?
- How did you organize your data on your chart? Did anyone use a different way of organizing your data?
- Describe the patterns you noticed in your data. Did a different way to organize the data cause different patterns to emerge? Explain.

Ask students to separate the data collected into two parts—data for cubes and data for other rectangular prisms. After students have reorganized their sets of data, ask them to compare and contrast them.

- How did the dimensions and volumes change in each of your cubes?
- How did the patterns help you to make and test conjectures about the volume of cubes?
- What do the patterns tell you about the relationship between the dimensions of a cube and its volume?
- Did you find the same patterns in the dimensions and volumes for your other prisms?
- If you know the volume of a cube, what do you have to know about it to determine its dimensions?
- Can you use the same strategy for finding the dimensions of other prisms when you know their volumes? Why or why not?

Follow-up Assessment Ideas

Offer students these challenges:

- Take one volume: sixty-four cubic units. List the dimensions of all possible rectangular prisms that can be built with that volume. Build or draw each prism to verify that its volume is sixty-four cubic units. How will you know you have found them all? Write about how you did your work and how you know you found all possible prisms with a volume of sixty-four cubic units.

- Write about how you used division in your volume investigations. What did you know? What were you trying to find? Which numbers did you use? Why?

Extension/Differentiation

Use the results of student work to decide which students might benefit from the following additional activities.

Investigation One: Hidden Hexahedra

Rationale: Students in research studies often look at pictures of solid shapes and find the volume by counting only the visible squares or cubes (Battista 2003). Experiences involving *inner invisible cubes* may enable students to move beyond this misconception. Have students follow the directions and answer the questions on the Task Card for Hidden Hexahedra (Figure H–3).

Investigation Two: Got You Covered!

Rationale: Because students tend to think of measurement as applying formulas rather than thinking about the number of squares that will cover a surface or the number of cubes that will fill a container, they need many different hands-on experiences finding volume and area to alleviate this confusion. Have students follow the directions and answer the questions on the task card for Got You Covered! (Figure H-4). Follow up by asking students to build prisms with a volume of sixty-four cubic units and record the surface areas of the prisms. Ask students to make conjectures about the prism with the least surface area and how this information might be used.

Hidden Hexahedra

■ Use interlocking cubes to build a larger cube with three units on an edge. How many cubes does it take? Do you notice that one cube is hidden by the other cubes no matter how hard you look for it?

■ How many inside cubes are hidden from view in a cube that is four units on an edge? Record your estimate first and then build the cube to find out.

■ How many cubes are hidden inside a cube that is five units on an edge?

■ Keep investigating different-sized cubes—recording each estimate first.

■ Organize your information. Do you notice any patterns? Describe them.

■ Do your patterns help you to predict the number of hidden cubes in larger cubes of any size? How?

Figure H–3   Task Card for Hidden Hexahedra   © 2010 by Jane F. Schielack and Dinah Chancellor from *Mathematics in Focus, K–6*. Portsmouth, NH: Heinemann.

Got You Covered!

■ Use the prisms you saved from "Prisms from Cubes" and add a third column to your data: "Surface Area." What new patterns do you uncover in your data?

■ Suppose you were to take a single volume, such as 24 cubic units. How many different rectangular prisms can you build with this volume? Do they all have the same surface area?

■ Choose two more volumes, such as 12 cubic units and 36 cubic units. Construct all possible prisms and find their surface areas. Describe the patterns in your data.

■ How do changes in dimensions affect surface area and volume?

Write about it.

Figure H–4 Task Card for Got You Covered! © 2010 by Jane F. Schielack and Dinah Chancellor from *Mathematics in Focus, K–6*. Portsmouth, NH: Heinemann.

Appendix 1:
Grade 6 Lesson Plan

Just Right!

Rationale and Objectives

Understanding the effects of maintaining a constant ratio between corresponding parts is the basis for understanding similarity and proportionality.

The student understands the following:

- A ratio is a comparison of two quantities.
- A ratio can compare two measurements.
- A ratio can be represented by a fraction.
- Equivalent ratios can be represented by equivalent fractions.
- To create objects with the same shape, you must maintain a constant ratio between the corresponding lengths of the two objects.

Materials

String, measuring tapes, yardsticks/meter sticks, grid paper (centimeter or inch), scissors, markers

Description of Activity

Students will use tools for measuring length and use constant ratios to create an object that is the same shape as, but a different size than, a given object (Figure I–1).

Procedure

Introduce

- Have students read a story that involves a small (or large) person or animal, such as *The Indian in the Cupboard* by Lynne Reid Banks or *Huge Harold* by Bill Peet.

- Have students discuss what it would be like to be much smaller or much larger than they are. What size would their desk need to be? What size would their clothes need to be? What size would their food need to be?

- Use the context of the story to present to students how to use the comparison of two numbers, a ratio, to describe the relative sizes of two objects. Use questions such as:

  - How tall is the Indian in the cupboard? How tall are you? How can we use multiplication to describe the relationship between your height and the Indian's height? [Note that students can use compatible numbers in the discussion to make the comparisons fairly simple. For example, the Indian is about six inches tall and an average sixth-grade student is five feet (60 inches) tall, so a student is ten times as tall as the Indian.]

  - How does the ratio sixty-to-six convey this same information? [A student's height compared to the Indian's height is sixty inches to six inches.]

  - Does ten-to-one describe the same comparison? [Yes; for every ten inches in the student's height, there is one inch in the Indian's height.]

- Explain to students that a comparison of two numbers is called a ratio and can be written as *60-to-6, 60:6*, or *60/6; 10-to-1, 10:1*, or *10/1*.

- Note that the ratio can also be thought of in the other order, comparing the Indian's height to a student's height. It is expressed as

Just Right!

You need: string, measuring tapes, rulers/meter sticks, grid paper (centimeter or inch), scissors, markers

■ Determine the ratio that describes the relationship between your character and a normal-sized person.

■ Use this ratio to build or draw an object for your character.

■ Record the measurements you use in the table.

■ Write about any patterns you observe.

Figure I–1   Task Card for Just Right!   © 2010 by Jane F. Schielack and Dinah Chancellor from *Mathematics in Focus, K–6*. Portsmouth, NH: Heinemann.

1/10, and it can be interpreted as the Indian is one-tenth the height of the student.

■ Discuss with students how they could use ratios to construct some object to be the appropriate size for the Indian in the cupboard, or for Harold the giant rabbit. Have students make a plan for creating the object, such as:

- Determine the ratio of the character to a normal-sized person. [There might be some decision making or research needed here as to what the measurement of a normal-sized person is and what particular aspect of the person to measure.]

- Record this ratio in a table like the one on the worksheet (Figure I–2) as a reference.

- Decide what object you want to make or draw for the character.

- Decide what lengths on the object you need to measure to be able to make or draw the object.

- Take a measurement of the normal-sized object and record it in the table.

- Use the ratio to decide what that length should be in the character's object and record it in the table.

- When you have enough measurements determined, use them to draw or make the character's object.

Explore

Have students work in pairs to build or draw an object for the character they choose (someone or something much smaller or larger than normal). As they proceed, focus their attention on the use of a constant ratio in their work. For embedded assessment, ask questions such as:

■ What did you decide the relationship of the two characters is?

■ How did you decide that?

■ How would you describe this relationship?

■ How did you record it in your table?

■ How are you using that relationship to find the measurements of the new object?

■ What do you notice about the measurements of the new object compared to the normal-sized object?

Recording Sheet for Just Right!

Measurement of:								
Normal object								
Character's object								

What is the ratio you used to describe the relationship between your character and a normal-sized person?

How did you use this ratio to find the measurements of the character's object?

What relationship is there between the measurements of the normal-sized object and the character's object?

What do you think would happen if you changed the ratio of one set of measurements?

Figure I–2   Recording Sheet for Just Right!   © 2010 by Jane F. Schielack and Dinah Chancellor from *Mathematics in Focus, K–6*. Portsmouth, NH: Heinemann.

Note: This activity can be differentiated based on the numbers the students choose to represent the relationship between the size of the character and the normal-sized person. For example, a ratio using actual measurements may turn out to be 9.75:1. Students may want to use calculators so they can focus on the relationships between the numbers.

Summarize

In the summary, have students discuss the data in their tables and their resulting object for the character. Focus students' attention on the relationship between the related measurements of the normal-sized object and the character's object:

- How did you use the ratio between the character and the normal-sized person to determine the measurements of your character's object?
- Did you use multiplication? If so, how?
- Did you use division? If so, how?
- Pick any pair of related measurements and divide one by the other. Now pick another pair of measurements and do the same thing. Do you get the same quotient? Why?
- What do you notice about your character's object? (It should look just the same, only smaller or larger.)
- Why do you think that happened?
- What do you think would happen if you changed the ratio in one of the pairs of related measurements?

Follow-up Assessment Ideas

Use the following problems to elicit evidence of understanding:

1. A certain car can travel 240 miles on a 16-gallon tank of gas. Create a ratio table to determine how many miles the car can travel on 1 gallon, 2 gallons, 3 gallons, 5 gallons, 12 gallons, x gallons.
2. Create a ratio table and use it to make a scale drawing of yourself to fit on a nine-by-twelve-inch piece of manila paper.
3. If the statue of Abraham Lincoln in the Lincoln Memorial in Washington, DC, could stand up, it would be approximately twenty-

eight feet tall. Create a ratio table that tells you what the lengths of your feet, hands, arms, legs would be if someone made a statue of you that was twenty-eight feet tall.

Extensions/Differentiation

Students can read *If You Hopped like a Frog* by David Schwartz and use ratios to determine how far they could hop if they hopped like a frog, or how wide they could open their mouth if they could swallow like a snake, or how much they could carry if they were as strong as an ant, and so forth. Students can use compatible number estimates for their ratios to make computation easier, or they can use more difficult numbers to represent their ratios to practice multiplication with fractions and decimals.

References

Anno, Mitsumasa. 1982. *Anno's Counting House*. New York: Philomel.

Baker, Keith. 1999. *Quack and Count*. Orlando: Harcourt.

Banks, Lynne Reid. 1980. *The Indian in the Cupboard*. New York: Avon Books.

Barnett, Carne, Donna Goldenstein, and Babette Jackson. 1994. *Mathematics Teaching Cases: Fractions, Decimals, Ratios, and Percents, Hard to Teach and Hard to Learn?* Portsmouth, NH: Heinemann.

Barrett, Jeffrey E., Graham Jones, Carol Thornton, and Sandra Dickson. 2003. "Understanding Children's Developing Strategies and Concepts for Length." In *Learning and Teaching Measurement*, edited by Douglas H. Clements, 17–30. Reston: National Council of Teachers of Mathematics.

Battista, Michael T. 2003. "Understanding Students' Thinking about Area and Volume Measurement." In *Learning and Teaching Measurement*, edited by Douglas H. Clements, 122–142. Reston, VA: National Council of Teachers of Mathematics.

Battista, Michael T. and Mary Berle-Carman. 1998. *Investigations in Number, Data, and Space: Containers and Cubes.* Menlo Park, CA: Dale Seymour Publications.

Battista, Michael T. and Douglas H. Clements. 1998. *Investigations in Number, Data, and Space: Exploring Solids and Boxes.* Menlo Park, CA: Dale Seymour Publications.

Chapin, Suzanne H. and Art Johnson. 2000. *Math Matters: Understanding the Math You Teach, Grades K–6.* Sausalito, CA: Math Solutions Publications.

CHARLESWORTH, ROSALIND. 2005. *Experiences in Math for Young Children* (5th ed.). Clifton Park, NY: Thomson Delmar Learning.

CLEMENTS, DOUGLAS H., JULIE SARAMA, eds., and ANN-MARIE DIBIASE, assoc. ed. 2004. *Engaging Young Children in Mathematics: Standards for Early Childhood Mathematics Education.* Mahwah, NJ: Lawrence Erlbaum.

COPLEY, JUANITA, ed. 1999. *Mathematics in the Early Years.* Reston, VA: National Council of Teachers of Mathematics.

———. 2004. *Showcasing Mathematics for the Young Child: Activities for Three-, Four-, and Five-Year-Olds.* Reston, VA: National Council of Teachers of Mathematics.

CORNING, PETER A. 2002. "The Re-emergence of 'Emergence': A Venerable Concept in Search of a Theory." *Complexity* 7 (6): 18–30.

FOSNOT, CATHERINE T. and MAARTEN DOLK. 2001a. *Young Mathematicians at Work: Constructing Multiplication and Division.* Portsmouth, NH: Heinemann.

———. 2001b. *Young Mathematicians at Work: Constructing Number Sense, Addition and Subtraction.* Portsmouth, NH: Heinemann.

———. 2002. *Young Mathematicians at Work: Constructing Fractions, Decimals, and Percents.* Portsmouth, NH: Heinemann.

FOX, STEPHEN. 1981. *John Muir and His Legacy: The American Conservation Movement.* Boston: Little, Brown, and Company.

FUSON, KAREN, LAURA GRANDAU, and PATRICIA A. SUGIYAMA. 2001. "Achievable Numerical Understandings for All Young Children." *Teaching Children Mathematics* 7 (9): 522–526.

GRIFFIN, SHARON. 2003. "Laying the Foundation for Computational Fluency in Early Childhood." *Teaching Children Mathematics* 9 (6): 306–309.

LAMON, SUSAN J. (1999). *Teaching Fractions and Ratios for Understanding: Essential Content Knowledge and Instructional Strategies for Teachers.* Mahwah, NJ: Erlbaum.

LAPPAN, GLENDA, JAMES FEY, WILLIAM FITZGERALD, SUSAN FRIEL, and ELIZABETH PHILLIPS. 1998. *Connected Mathematics—Filling and Wrapping: Three-Dimensional Measurement.* Menlo Park, CA: Dale Seymour Publications.

LITWILLER, BONNIE, ed. 2002. *Making Sense of Fractions, Ratios, and Proportions.* Reston, VA: National Council of Teachers of Mathematics.

MERRIAM, EVE. 1993. *12 Ways to Get to 11.* New York: Simon & Schuster.

NATIONAL COUNCIL OF TEACHERS OF MATHEMATICS. 2000. *Principles and Standards for School Mathematics.* Reston, VA: National Council of Teachers of Mathematics.

————. 2006. *Curriculum Focal Points for Prekindergarten through Grade 8 Mathematics: A Quest for Coherence.* Reston, VA: National Council of Teachers of Mathematics.

NATIONAL MATHEMATICS ADVISORY PANEL. 2008. *Foundations for Success: The Final Report of the National Mathematics Advisory Panel.* Washington, DC: U.S. Department of Education.

PARISH, PEGGY. 1963. *Amelia Bedelia.* New York: HarperCollins.

PAYNE, JOSEPH N., ed. 1990. *Mathematics for the Young Child.* Reston, VA: National Council of Teachers of Mathematics.

PEET, BILL. 1961. *Huge Harold.* New York: Houghton Mifflin.

RICHARDSON, KATHY. 2002. *Assessing Math Concepts: The Hiding Assessment.* Rowley, MA: Didax.

ROSS, SHARON. 1989. "Parts, Wholes, and Place Value: A Developmental View." *Arithmetic Teacher* 36 (6): 47–51.

SCHIELACK, JANE F., DINAH CHANCELLOR, and KIM CHILDS. 2000. "Designing Questions to Encourage Children's Mathematical Thinking." *Teaching Children Mathematics* 6 (6): 398–402.

SCHIELACK, JANE F. and DINAH CHANCELLOR. 1995. *Uncovering Mathematics with Manipulatives and Calculators.* Dallas, TX: Texas Instruments.

SHROYER, JANET and WILLIAM FITZGERALD. 1986. *Middle Grades Mathematics Project—Mouse and Elephant: Measuring Growth.* Menlo Park, CA: Addison-Wesley.

STEPS PROFESSIONAL DEVELOPMENT AUSTRALIA. 2007a. *First Steps in Mathematics, Measurement, Volume 1.* Perth, Western Australia: Edith Cowan University.

————. 2007b. *First Steps in Mathematics, Number, Volume 1.* Perth, Western Australia: Edith Cowan University.

STURGES, PHILEMON. 1995. *Ten Flashing Fireflies.* New York: North-South Books.

SCHWARTZ, DAVID. 1999. *If You Hopped Like a Frog.* New York: Scholastic Press.

VAN DE WALLE, JOHN A. 2007. *Elementary and Middle School Mathematics: Teaching Developmentally* (6th ed.). Boston: Pearson.